JAMILAH J THOMAS

Artasque

Second edition

ISBN: 979-8-218-26742-1

Cover art by Ashley Siebels

This book was professionally typeset on Reedsy.
Find out more at reedsy.com

Contents

1

On display - chapter 1

An art critic who was never labeled an artist, made hundreds by sending in good scores on artwork. The art critic was June Flamingo. She had finally made it into the limelight as someone who gave some of the most honest critics of time. After working behind the scenes as an assistant for 5 years, she got her masters while studying art education.

On a windy Thursday afternoon in 1995, she was in the middle of New York. June Flamingo was currently taking a taxi to go see the newest art exhibit in the city. June stared out the window, looking at the busy four o'clock traffic, hoping she would make it in time before the art exhibit closed. "You're June Flamingo, a famous critic; my daughter tells me all about you, do you live here?" the driver asked while taking a sip of his water at the stop sign. "No, I'm just visiting. I actually live in Las Vegas," she said loudly, trying to be heard over the busy traffic. The driver nodded and said, "Is your last name really based on a bird?", with a thick New York accent with a curious tone in his voice. June responded with a nervous "yes, it is based off the bird" before staring in silence out the window. It wasn't the first time she had been asked that question. June knew it was going to be a long car ride to the exhibit.

June Flamingo closed her eyes for what felt like more than a minute when the car suddenly came to a halt. June paid the driver ten dollars to drive her to the exhibit. Then she offered to actually send a face-to-face video to his daughter. "She is going to be so excited," he said with a grin on his face while waving at her while driving off. June was a little tense and excited, but she straightened up as she looked behind her at the exhibit. With one deep breath, she started walking towards the exhibit doors. As she got closer, she could almost hear the number of people in the exhibit. June took a quick peek before deciding if she should walk in late. Everyone inside seemed to dress formally. June was wearing a blue turtleneck with black stripes on the top and her sleeves, and she paired it with a black long skirt. The boots that she brought with her on this trip brought the whole outfit together. June walked inside the exhibit and looked around as if it was her first time on the job.

After gazing through the exhibit, she felt more at ease with herself than at the beginning. The exhibit was to honor a few famous artists of the time, and some of them were known to be European. June hasn't seen European art in person since traveling to Italy during her college years. She decided it was time to go back to the hotel, so she started walking back to the door. Until she stopped in front of a painting, she seemed to have missed It was a huge painting of a beautiful pale lady with a green dress, and it seemed like classical paintings inspired the artist. June was so stunned by the beauty of the painting, that she forgot the exhibit was about to close in a few moments. The thing that brought her back to reality was a freshly combed man in a black suit standing next to her. "It's a beautiful painting," he said in truthful tone with a Italian accent while looking at June. June looked around for in the direction the voice came from until she saw the man standing next to her. "Oh, lord, was I standing here for long?" she said, almost frightened by his sudden appearance. He reassured her that she was fine, and he told her he worked for the exhibit. "If you like the painting so much, buy it," he said in eager tone sprinkled with teasing motives, waiting for her to respond with a wide grin. June laughed at the thought of buying such a expensive painting until she saw that he was serious. "There's an auction in two days, and this painting is going to be in it." The man said to June in a honest tone. The artist passed away last week." The man added with some sadness in his voice. June replied with concern, "I didn't know, how did a French painting get here?" While looking at the painting, she turned her head to see that the man had vanished. In utter shock, he would leave her like that, with no answer but also curious about this upcoming auction. June decided that since she would be in New York for another week, she would attend the auction. Since June didn't have much money to spend, she would come to watch. The strange thing was, why would he answer all of her questions but disappear before answering her last one?

2

Lady in Green - chapter 2

Eddison Blackburn started his career as a business owner until one of his past co-workers scammed him. After that, he turned to a life of crime, which made him one of the richest people in the world. Eddison would travel around the world and scam people for their money and also he had a few of them murdered in return. Eddison knows that his work isn't original in this era, but he believes he has come a long way since working for other Wall Street workers. "Boss, I have some news," his accomplice, Alex Dunn, told him. Alex Dunn was holding a newspaper with an excited smile. Blackburn stopped sipping his coffee and looked up with a brooding face at Alex. He took that as a sign to tell him, "A painter just died in his apartment; see, look." Alex holded up the newspaper. Eddison read from the newspaper while touching his full black beard. "I believe you're right." "What, do you want to go to their funeral?" he smirked at Alex. Alex scoffed at his reply, knowing Eddison could never take him seriously.

Alex was a few years younger than Eddison and newer to the business. Alex's hands went through his bright orange hair as he thought of the best reply. "It just reminds me a lot about the Flaminos," Alex huffed. Eddison chuckled at Alex being mad at him for not understanding why he would bring up the death. Eddison is smart, so he got it as soon as he told him. "You want us to steal a painting?" he asked Alex with a sly smile. He got up from the dining chair he was sitting in and walked towards his office. Alex rambled about how he should play a part in this heist since he's younger, and Eddison ignored him because he was always going to play a part. Eddison pulled out his Mac computer and typed in the painter's name into the web search box. He looked through the paintings that the artist had made, and he found one that stuck out to him.

"A lady in a green dress?" Alex questioned the painting choice among many of the better options. Eddison got up from his seat, and Alex jumped at the sudden height difference. Eddison replied, "Yes, but it's called Untitled from what I saw." Eddison explained they were going to trick the museum in France into thinking that the painter's brother wanted the painting moved to a random New York convention. The plan worked out as planned with no struggles and they were able to trick them. The painting took about a month to get officially into the exhibit, which took a week to be officially set up. Then the day came, the year was 1995, and it was time for the painting to be shown off at the exhibit. "Sir, "Aren't we going to steal?-" Eddison interrupted Alex by putting his hand over his mouth. The two of them were currently standing near the painting they were planning to steal. Eddison uncovered his mouth and replied, "You know we are stealing it at the auction; remember the plan."

Alex nodded at Eddison while almost readjusting his mouth from Eddison's hard hand grip. A few of the visitors were walking around the exhibit until one of them caught Eddison's attention. The person was June Flamingo, an art critic who was visiting from Las Vegas. "Sir, do you mind telling me who made this painting?" She asked a worker. June was staring at a more abstract painting with a lot of colorful dots. The men overheard June speaking about how the exhibit was very diverse, with many different styles. "It's truly amazing; I enjoy New York exhibits." June smiled at the worker. The worker waved as they walked away to speak with another attendant. June had made her way through the hall to meet face-to-face with one painting. The painting was hung up on the wall alone, and there were two hallways on both sides of it. It was almost like there was a spotlight shining on it. Eddison watched as she looked at the painting. June's eyes began to water as she was reminded of someone dear to her. Eddison was overwhelmed by all the emotion, so he adjusted his suit and began walking out towards June.

He let her have her moment with the painting before trying to get her back to reality. "It's a beautiful painting!" He shouted only slightly. June looked to her side to realize that he had been standing there watching her admire the painting. Eddison decided to tell her that the auction would be happening in a few days. "I can't believe you would tell her you work there," Alex said, shocked. Eddison took off his fake employee ID and handed it to Alex before saying, "I'm adding her to the plan." Alex was confused about why he would add an art critic who he had just met. "What are you going to do?" "Use her as bait?" Alex shouted, as Eddison was already near the car. Eddison stopped in his tracks and realized what he was about to get her into. He walked back towards Alex. "She's not going to be in the heist or doing a heist," he chuckled.

The two men got into their cars and started driving away from the exhibit. A few days ago, Alex called the exhibit to let them know that the painting was there to be sold at the next auction as a way of getting rid of the paintings after the artist had died. Alex was able to convince them that he was the brother of the artist who wanted the paintings sold as soon as possible. "I'm sorry, I can't possibly come." "I'm still mourning the loss of my dear brother," Alex had said that morning, using his fake French accent with a combination of fake crying. Once the painting was auctioned off, they would sneak behind the curtains and steal it. "So what if we're caught?" Alex said this while driving the black car to the apartment they were currently staying at. "We aren't the ones that are going to be caught," Eddison reassured him while lighting a cigarette as Alex stopped at a stop sign. Eddison has never been caught in all his years of crime, and he thought that this would be no different. "So we're framing her?" Alex gasped as if he could read Eddison's mind.

"Do you know who that is?" Eddison asked before taking a puff of his cigarette.

Alex didn't respond as he thought of who June could possibly be. "Um, she's an art critic," Alex responded with a confused look at Eddison. Eddison rolled the window up before saying, "That's June Flamingo!" He told Alex. Alex gave another confused look before turning the wheel. "But, Eddison, you already told me about her." Eddison interrupted him by explaining that someone else has the name June. "Remember when you brought up the Flaminos?" Eddison asked Alex. Alex nodded, having no idea where this could possibly go. "Um, is she related or something?" Eddison sighed, his hands rubbing against his face. "Yes, she's related; she's their daughter," Eddison responded with a frustrated look at Alex. Alex was still driving, so he couldn't see his boss's face at the time. Eddison blurted out at him, saying, "That's June Flamino; she changed her damn name."

3

Curtains open - chapter 3

"So she changed her name after her parents died?" Alex plummeted while turning the car off. Eddison clarified that when she got older, she changed her name. "So we're framing her because her parents were famous?" Alex questioned Eddison's plan. Eddison walked to the other side of the car and stood in front of Alex. "Everyone in this world thinks that June's dead, and this is a new June." Eddison burned out his cigar. "Think about the story…" "A young girl gets back at the media for getting rid of her after her parents' deaths—" Alex interrupted me to finish his sentence, "by stealing a painting." Eddison patted Alex on the shoulder for finally understanding what he was talking about. The two of them walked into the apartment, and Eddison looked behind him to see if anyone was watching him.

In June's hotel room, she changed into her sleepwear before turning on the nightly news. She thought about what the mysterious man had said to her at the exhibit about the auction coming in two years. A plane ticket home was already scheduled for that Sunday, so it wouldn't be much of a change if she went. June layed on the bed as she changed the channel to see if any movies were on. She pulled out a brush to brush her curly brown hair, when she got to a channel that was playing *Reservoir Dogs*. "Oh, I haven't seen this in a while," June said to herself as she got under the covers. On the days before the auction, she would go shopping for an outfit for the auction. She didn't bring anything formal that would work, but she didn't want to make any excuses for not dressing up.

At one store in the mall, she found a long-sleeve coat with a pair of black pants and a black beret to match. Until it came to the day of the auction, which she learned was scheduled for four o'clock on Saturday. At two o'clock, she prepared herself for the auction. She heard at one of the pizza places she stopped at that it was going to be a black-tie event. June applied black nail polish and red lipstick. She straightened her hair so her beret wouldn't fall off. Then she put on her black boots to finish the outfit. After looking at herself in the mirror, she was ready to call a taxi to the auction at around three o'clock. The taxi driver was silent except for when she paid for her ride at the end. The driver helped her out of the taxi since they saw she was wearing higher boots. June would wear higher shoes to these types of events to present herself better, even though she was of average height.

June showed the man who was showing people inside her ID. "Ah, June Flamingo, the auction hall is to your left." The man pointed in the direction of the auction hall. The doors of the auction hall were already opened, so she stepped inside the room. The auction room was large and filled with many circle tables that were almost filled with tons of people. June thought that most of these people must be here for the grand painting that the public was told was being auctioned here only a few days ago. The auction looked like it was reaching its maximum capacity of how many people could be in there. June looked behind her to see groups of people coming in, so she thought it was best if she found a seat. June chose the table all the way to the back of the room, near the door. An older lady was speaking with a guy about how there was a mistake with her seating. The man seemed to look like he had just gotten done walking a cross-country race, and June concluded he had been a worker that night. "Can we sit here?" A lady wearing a mint-colored top with a scarf asked June. June nodded, as it was too loud for her to be heard. The group sat next to June while she looked at the front, where they brought out the first painting that was going to be auctioned.

The speaker tapped on his microphone before saying, "Excuse me, I will be your host for this year's annual auction." The crowd cheered because the auction had begun. June watched the auction go by incredibly fast. The first painting that was up was a painting of a woman's body that was almost abstract, and the second one was an upside-down house. The time had finally come for what the majority had been waiting for; the painting of the lady in the green dress. "Going for 1 million," the speaker said out towards the crowd. June watched as two men fought over the painting and listened as the price went up. They realized they had not brought the painting up. June thought it was because the painting was very expensive. She saw an orange-haired man walk towards where she was sitting. "Ma'am, I'm going to need you to come with me," he whispered to her. She stood up, wondering if something had happened. The man led her to a seat all the way in front. When she sat down, she made eye contact with the lady she had just heard complaining about seats. June coughed under her breath before turning to look at the speaker and not questioning the sudden seat change. The speaker handed the microphone to the person who had just led her to her new seat. The art critic could hear the collective confusion of everyone in the auction hall as the man spoke. "I'm sorry, but I have great news," said the man, who was named Alex Dunn.

"Since the anniversary of the death of the Flaminos is coming," Alex paused so he could move a piece in his hair, almost like he was trying to hear something. June suddenly sat up straighter than she already was before realizing what last name he had just said. Her hands become sweaty thinking about his next words. "I wanted to bring a special guest; please welcome June Flamino," Alex yelled through the microphone as he pointed at June. The auction hall started clapping for June and chanting her name. Alex waved her up to the stage to say a few words. June stepped up slowly in front of the light. The large room in front of her looked less crowded than before, and the bright light shone on her face. She looked to her right to find that Alex was gone. June began, "Thank you," as the crowd became silent. "I have had such a journey with my career," she added before hearing a big crash behind her. The curtains of the red velvet auction hall had dramatically fallen down to reveal the backstage. June heard gasps, screams, and confusion all in front of her. June slowly turned around to see that the curtains were down and the painting was down. Something that no one in the audience could see was the backstage door being opened. June mumbled something under her breath. The audience started yelling at June to get off the stage. "Thief," "She's getting back at us for her parents' death," and "You're no art critic!" are the words that she heard from the room. June tried to say something, but nothing came out of her mouth. The security guards started walking toward the stage. June started running for the backstage door. One security guard caught her in her tracks, but he let her go. She called for a taxi as soon as she got outside. "Dang girl, did you commit a crime," the taxi driver said as he pulled off from the auction hall. June breathed heavily as she replied in her mind, "No, but I was framed for one." As soon as she got to her hotel building, she kicked off her boots. June had lost her beret back at the auction hall, but she was glad to be alive. The next morning she had a plane to catch.

4

Video links - chapter 4

The year is 2000 as I am in front of my television in my parents' apartment in Las Vegas, Nevada. I am watching the news at 10 in the morning. I don't like to leave the house because I feel like people will try to say horrible things to me. Ever since the auction, people have not taken me seriously. While I haven't quit my career yet but, I don't criticize artwork as much anymore. Suddenly, I heard a knock at the door while I was watching television. I turned down the television and yelled, "Who is it?". I thought that it would be my drug-dealing neighbor who had just moved across from me. He said that he would keep my location a secret if I didn't tell the police what he had stored in his apartment. I remembered that he was probably on one of his sprees this early in the morning.

After a while, the knocking stopped, so I went into my room to get dressed. With quickness, I threw on a brown collared long sleeve shirt with black pants. Then I picked a pair of sneakers from my closet. Honestly, I didn't plan on leaving the house today, or so I thought. After I got dressed, I went into the kitchen to make a bowl of cereal. My thirty-fourth birthday was last month and celebrated at home alone. I haven't had much luck with friendships because I'm somewhat wanted right now. I don't have much luck with relationships because most people I went to school with didn't leave Las Vegas, either. My reputation was ruined once my old last name was revealed to the public. They didn't like that I didn't have the artistic skills like my parents, so the public threw me to the wolves.

Feeling cautious, I finished my bowl of cereal, cleaned my bowl, and sat back down in front of the TV. I would text my boss, but I don't have one anymore. I am currently making money by rating people's artwork anonymously. Even though my neighbor told me last week that the drug dealing business made him rich. But people already think I'm an untalented thief. I wouldn't want to add drug dealing to the list of things to get arrested for. While I get as comfortable as possible to sit on my coach for the rest of the day, I hear another knock on the door. But this time it's louder. I get up to turn off the television. I put on my sneakers before walking towards the door. "I know it's you, stop playing with me" I yelled through the door. I unlocked my door and turned the knob. "So what is it you what–" I said before realizing that it was actually an FBI agent knocking on the door the whole time.

"Are you June Flamino?" he said, reading a paper in his hand. I rubbed the back of my head before looking up at him, since he was twice my height. "No, I'm June Flamingo," I denied while my hands became clammy from the thought of probably going to jail. "Isn't this the Flamino residence? '' He asked me with a confused look on his face. We both looked at each other for what seemed like minutes before he had no choice but to take me in. I wonder if he could sense my nervous behavior. "June Flamino, I'm taking you in for suspicion for the stealing of the painting at the New York auction of 1995", he said while grabbing my arm. I looked out my window near the kitchen, but I knew it was pointless. His grip was already pulling me through the hallways and into the elevators. Before I knew it, I was already in the car being taken to the station to be asked questions against my will. But, I would not be going to prison or at least I would hope not.

When we got to the station, he told me to wait in an interrogation room. My legs began to shake, and my face became sweaty. I knew this was going to happen someday. I was unprepared for the interrogation to happen on this day. Since I didn't brush down my hair before I would be dragged out of the apartment, my hair was in my face. So I pulled a hair tie out of my pocket to turn my hair into a ponytail. I was waiting for whoever was going to talk to me for almost an hour. I was about to close my eyes before I saw the man who looked to be the detective. The detective went over to me and shook my hand firmly. "I'm sorry; we had to bring you here that way," he apologized. I put my hand down on the table and straightened my back. The Detective pulled out a small, square television on a roller. He took two cassettes from his jacket pocket, then took his jacket off. He placed his jacket on the seat in front of him. I watched him as he put one of the cassettes on the television. I quivered at the thought of what footage he might be using against me. I shook my head to try to shake the nerves out of me. I needed to prove I was innocent because I was innocent.

"Ms. Flamino, I would like to ask you a few questions," he said with a slight smile to ease the tension in the small room. I nodded, thinking that I wished he would use my current last name. "Do you remember what you were doing at the New York art exhibit in 1995?" He asked me. The television flashed static as he hadn't pushed play on any clips yet. "I was there to leave reviews on the art in the exhibit," I replied.

He pushed play on the television, and the video that played seemed to be playback from exhibit cameras. "Ms. Flamino, are you looking at the painting that is missing?" the detective asked.

"Yes," I replied. The detective pressed the fast-forward button on the television. "Do you know the man who you are talking to at this point in the video?" he added. My hands were in my lap, and suddenly my legs stopped shaking. "No, I did not know him," I said to him.

"What is it he said to you?" he asked. I thought for a moment before saying, "I don't remember." I added, "I mean, he invited me to the auction." He pulled out a notebook from under the stand where the television was on. I noticed when he would write my answers quickly. "Ms. Flamino, are you aware that we spoke with some of the auction holders of that year?" he said before flipping a page in his notebook. "I meant with everyone, and no one looked like this man," he said while looking at what could have been the names of the auction runners of that year.

He put in the video footage of the auction. "Do you know this man?" he asked, pointing at a man on the screen with orange hair. "No, I don't," I replied, making direct eye contact. "A lady told me they saw you move a seat because of him; is this correct?" he asked me while writing something else in his small notebook. "Yes, that is correct. The person directed me to a different seat," I said, moving my hands to the side of the body.

"Well, that's all the questions I have," he said before getting up from his chair in front of me. It was almost watching him walk away in slow motion. I realized that he only asked me questions that somehow revolved around my knowing those men. I realized they were going to use my last answer. "Wait!" I screamed with one hand on the table. The detective stopped in his tracks right before he was going to open the door. He didn't turn around when he heard me. "Are you suggesting that because they saw me interacting with them?" I said in an angry tone, huffing, trying to catch my breath from sweating in the overly hot room. "It means that I stole it!" I questioned the detective's mindset.

The detective turned around and put his notebook in his jacket pocket. "You were running from the security, which didn't help you much," he said while making eye contact with me. I would set back down in my chair before saying, "What was I supposed to do? I wasn't the person who stole the painting." In an annoyed tone. He looked around the room before walking really close to me. "Prove it," he told me with a smile on his face, like he was trying to make a bet with me. I looked down at the table until I realized, "Fine, I will try to get the painting back," I said while standing up from my chair to match his height. I didn't know where those men were. The painting had been missing for a while. I wasn't sure if I was going to get the painting back. After a couple of minutes of him talking to his colleagues, he let me go. But he said he wanted me to do one thing: "Don't leave your house; stop doing your career."

While I was walking out of the station, I saw a younger girl sitting in one of the waiting chairs. She had golden, messy blonde hair, freckles, and tan skin. She was wearing a mint top with jeans. I waved at her, even though she didn't wave back at me. I didn't question why she was at the police station, but I was ready to leave that place. Since I was being forced to quit my job, I would have a lot of time to be in the apartment to think about everything.

5

Teenage girlhood - chapter 5

Valerie Wood will turn 18 tomorrow. Instead of partying with her teenage friends, she was at the police station, waiting to be taken home by her father. Her father worked at the police station in Las Vegas. The teenager had been home schooled at a very young age because her mother didn't trust the school environment with her daughter. Valerie did not have any friends her age because of this. She watched as June left the station after her meeting. "Is she serious?" her dad asked the detective. Her dad was talking about June, saying that she could get the painting back to prove she was innocent. The detective showed her dad his notes. The two of them walked into a room, and Valeria could still make out what they were saying.

Her dad walked out of the room with the detective. He made a hand signal to let her know he was ready to leave. As they were walking to the car, Valeria sensed that something was watching them. "Val, are you okay?" Her dad said this while turning around to face her. Valeria looked behind her to see if anyone was watching her. She sighed. "No, I'm tired," she said while running to catch up with her dad, who was already in the car. Her dad chuckled. "It's only four o'clock," he said while looking at his watch. "It's just so tiring sitting in a plastic chair for an hour," she said while dramatically putting her hand on her forehead. "Who was that woman, anyway?" she asked her father as he started pulling out of the station parking lot. He started humming to the music, as if he couldn't hear what she had said. Valeria was about to repeat herself until he said, "A woman," with a smile on his face. "Dad, I know that's June Flamingo," she said while looking out the window. Her dad did a full-belly laugh because she used June's other last name.

Valeria asked no more questions because she knew her dad wouldn't give any answers. He would not answer questions about June, the painting, or the auction. Her dad pulled into the driveway of the house. Valeria asked, "Why did you ask me to come to the station if you weren't going to tell me anything?" Her dad sighed, rubbed Valeria's shoulder, and then opened the door. "Top secret, and you're not good at keeping those." Her dad said this while walking toward her from outside the car. Valeria got out of the car, closed her door, and they walked towards the house. Valeria opened the door to the house only to meet face-to-face with one of her dad's secrets.

"Surprise!" screamed her mother while standing in front of a homemade cake. Her mother was about to fall into it, but Valeria and her father caught her. "Mom, watch the icing!" Valeria said while helping her stand back up. They all enjoyed the cake that her mother had made for her eighteenth birthday. "What are your plans for the rest of the year?" Her dad said this while stuffing his face with cake. Valeria finished eating the cake she already had in her mouth before saying, "I want to apply to my dream college." Valeria responded excitedly. Her parents both looked at each other. "What?" Valeria said, while her smile faded. Her parents looked at each other again, like they were telepathy who should speak first.

"Sweetheart," her dad said, while putting his fork down. "Yesterday, your mother found out we lost a lot of money," he added while holding her mother's hand. Valeria's eyes widened with confusion. "All of it?" Valeria asked both of them. The two of them nodded their heads without saying a word. The three of them sat in silence until Valeria broke it with, "Okay." Her dad looked at her mom. "So you're not mad," he said while trying to force a smile. Valeria got up to put her plate in the sink. She turned around to say, "No, I'm not."

"We will be okay," she said, then walked away. She slowly made her way to her room, and then she jumped onto her bed.

"We will not be okay," she said while shaking her head at her co-worker four days after her parents told her what happened. "All this robbery lately—is it a trend or something?" her younger co-worker said while laughing. Valeria worked at one of the car wash stops near her house. Even though it was a stressful job, it paid her a lot of money. Specifically, when the casino owners go to wash their car. After finishing washing a car, she tells her co-worker, "It's been days since they brought that up." Her co-worker quickly responded, "And you're just going to act like your family doesn't with no money in name."

A car pulled in front of Valeria. It looked like it cost a lot of money. She knew that's where the good money comes from. The driver rolled down his window to give her the money. She put the money in her pocket, not noticing that he gave her a business card as well. After the car pulled off, she opened the money roll to find a stack of hundreds and the card. Her eyes widened as she watched the car pull off from the car wash.

When she was on break, she called the number on the card. "Hello?" she asked through the phone. The person on the other side didn't respond. Valeria said, "It says on the card you were in the need of workers." She looked around her as she stood at the back of a building near the car wash. "I really need the money for college," she said, holding back tears. "I'll do anything," she added while holding her phone close to her. The phone was silent for a second until she thought that the person had hung up on her. "Get the painting back; I will give you the money," the voice on the other end of the phone said, sounding like they were almost standing far away from the phone. "What! How! Who are you?" she screamed, forgetting she was still in public.

She bent down on the concrete floor while waiting for an answer. "You will receive a letter in 8 days max." "Open it," the person said before hanging up. "Wait! You didn't tell me who you were," Valeria said, holding herself up from the concrete floor. Tears went down her face while she spoke through the phone. "I can't wait 8 days!" I can't!". Her co-worker was standing behind her for a minute until they came to get her off the floor. Her co-worker picked her up and dragged her over their shoulder. "You should probably clean your hands before cleaning any cars," they said while laughing. Valeria was emotionless while hanging over their shoulders.

Valeria was thinking about who that person on the other end was. She knew it couldn't have been the person who had the car she washed. But she knew what painting he was talking about. "By the way, I'm going to see some wrestling tomorrow night." Her co-worker paused for a second, thinking about what to say next. Her co-worker was the same age as her, and had been friend zoned multiple times by Woods since she joined the team. "Would you like to come?" her co-worker added. Valeria snapped back to reality when she heard what they said. She replied, "Yes." Before her coworker could squeal in excitement, her other coworker screamed, "Stop flirting in public!"

6

Champion - chapter 6

Valerie Wood looked to see that the time was six pm. Her co-worker was about to pick her up for a date tonight to see a wrestling match. She put on some chopstick and grabbed her purse. Her outfit consisted of a green tank top, jeans, and black sandals. While checking to see if she had any money in her purse, she heard her mother talking to her father. "I can't believe you're gambling again," her mother said, putting her hands to her face in distress. Valeria's father put his hand on her shoulder, but she pushed his hand off. "We literally lost our money because of your sick games," she added with a furious look on her face. Valeria was peeking from around the corner while this was all happening. She made herself known, as she felt like the argument was about to escalate.

Valeria's dad turned her head to see her walking towards the door from the hallway across from the kitchen. "Oh, I didn't see you." "Be safe!" her dad said while walking towards the hallway to almost catch up to her. Valeria was already outside, so she couldn't hear him. She was holding her purse on the porch, waiting for her coworker to pull in front of the house. Her co-worker speeds in front of the house to come to a stop. He parks his coverless car, then runs over to Valeria. "OM, I'm so sorry," he panicked while grabbing Valeria's hand. She was emotionless as he pulled her through the yard until she chuckled, "Chill for a second; we aren't late." He stopped pulling her, and before he could apologize again, she added, "Let's just go before my parents think you're kidnapping me." He moved his head to see her parents looking out the window, and he nodded.

Valeria and her co-worker got into the car. They put their seat belts on, and he pulled the car off the house. He asked, "Do you like any music?" Valeria took a second to answer because no one had asked her that question for a long time. Before she could answer, he had switched to a channel that had just started playing *Semi-Charmed Life by Third Eye Blind.* Valeria looked at her co-worker, who still had his hand on the radio switch. "I like this song," she said while moving his hand from the switch so he could drive faster to the wrestling match. The parking lot of the place where the match was being held was packed. Her co-worker had already bought tickets, so they didn't need to pay upfront.

The two of them sat in the middle of the left side of the match with perfect viewing. Valeria overheard people talking about how the match was going to start, but this was her first time going to see a wrestling match. She stood up to see what was going on. She sat back down and looked at her co-worker to say, "Your name's James, right?" He was already eating his popcorn, so he ate what he had in his mouth before saying, "Yes, that's my name." The match didn't start until 10 minutes later, at around 7:35 p.m. She heard a microphone being tested, so she knew it was about to start. A man went into the arena with a microphone in his hand. He said, "Welcome!" "Now let's get this started, shall we?"

Everything went really fast for Valeria because she wasn't used to this type of air. At some points in the match, her co-worker explained the different moves the wrestlers were doing on each other. But one thing that Valeria remembered was that one of them was a champion wrestler. "So he's won 15 total matches in a row?" Valeria asked James while screaming for him to hear her. James explained that this wrestler has competed since his 20s, and he hasn't stopped since. The wrestler was named Caddock House; he was dark-skinned with black hair. He had a muscular body, but it looked natural. House's 15-year streak would be broken that night. "1, 2, 3," the man said, and then he held up the wrestler's hand. The hand of whom was not Caddock House's, Valeria could hear a mixture of boos and cheers.

James sensed the tension in the crowd, so he touched Valeria's arm to get her attention. "I think it's about to get rowdy; I'll drive you home," he said while getting up. The two of them made their way to the exit while the crowd did indeed get rowdy.

Caddock was behind the scenes, getting ready to get out of his wrestling clothes, when his manager knocked on the door. Caddock opened the door with a jacket and shorts on. "What, are you going to fire me now?" he fumed at his manager. The two of them have never had the best relationship. Caddock's manager was the reason he could never see his child, so his girlfriend broke up with him. The manager promoted a fake relationship between House and a model for clout. His manager thought about cutting his paycheck if he lost this match. "I'm the one paying you," his manager said.

"I'm only here because I won't give up on my passion," Caddock argued. His manager laughed, saying, "Admit it, you liked the attention you got from that streak." "There is nothing to be admitted; you're working me to death," he yelled. The door to his dressing room was still open when he raised his voice. He put his hand on the mirror desk. "Is this about a fake relationship?" his manager asked with a sly smile. Caddock clenched his jaw, thinking about all the outcomes of getting paid back for what his manager did. Instead, he thought about the only option possible. He was going to go out with a bang. "I quit," he said, while he grabbed his bags and walked out of the building.

Valeria didn't want to go out with a bang. Valeria's co-worker dropped her off around eleven p.m. that night. She thanked him for the amazing night and even gave him a hug. But not the kiss he was hoping for, in comparison to those romance movies. "Thank you; you're such a great friend," she said while patting his shoulder. She walked towards the house, and she could almost hear the shocked look on his face. Before she turned in the keys to the house, she heard crying coming from inside. She turned the doorknob and ran into the house. She didn't have to run fast before seeing her mother on the kitchen floor in the same outfit she saw her in early that day. The confused teenager kneeled down on the floor at her mother's level. "Mom, where's dad?" she said, confused as she didn't have any physical signs of a fight.

Her mom stuttered. "He went out gambling again," she said as she wiped her eyes. Valeria's eyes watered as she thought of her father's gambling addiction and her mother's love for her father. "Mom," she said to her mother as she helped her stand up from the floor. "I'm done telling dad he's fine; he's not!" she said to her mother. She sighed while looking down before saying, "I quit."

7

Paintings on fire - chapter 7

It was a windy summer day in Las Vegas. June Flamingo was picking out an outfit to wear to a conference she was invited to this morning to ask questions, even though the detective stated that she shouldn't do public events until the case was closed. She pulled out a hair straightener to straighten her hair for the event. This would be her first public event in a long time. She walked out of the apartment door in a red turtleneck paired with a brown skirt and a formal jacket. She called a taxi to take her to the event center. When she got in, she told them the address and placed her purse next to her. After putting her seat belt on, she realized that the taxi driver looked familiar. The taxi driver looked in his mirror. "your June Flamingo," he said while turning out of the apartment complex parking lot. "Did your daughter get the video?" June said this while remembering that he asked for a video for his daughter a few years ago. "Oh, she loved it and showed it to all her friends," he said.

June thought about how, five years ago, she was liked among younger people. Teens dreamed of being as loved as she was in her career field and wanted to be criticized by her. She was now disliked by people of the same demographic. She thought about how the times had changed. The ride went by really fast, mostly because it was the middle of the day on a Monday. "You know most people I pick up are hung over at a party from Sunday," he laughed while stopping at a red light. June replied, "Who says I'm not hung over?" while laughing to let him know she was joking. He pulled in front of the event center, which was packed with possible critics ready to force-feed her questions. She opened the back door, realizing she had forgotten to pay him. June pulled out a ten-dollar bill to give him money for the ride, but he shook his head. "The rides on me." "You're like a household name, Flamingo," he said while smiling. She was shocked as he pulled away from the event center.

After asking so many people where to go, June was being taken to the front of the room, where the audience would be. She had a microphone set up in front of her, and the room was going to be filled with reporters. June thought that she wished she was in a press room for a movie or a new album. The press questions went by one by one as she sighed before answering every question. All revolved around her stealing the painting, quitting her career, or going to jail, as she expected. The lights gleamed brightly on June's face. All the cameras flashed in all different directions, showing different angles of June from one seat. The noises of different voices meshed together, even though every reporter had a microphone of their own.

Before she was going to answer another question from a United Kingdom reporter, she put up her hand. "Is she asking to stop?" she heard someone from the crowd say. She was putting her hand over one of the camera lights when something else caught her eye. A girl was leaning up against the wall in the back of the room. June rubbed her eyes for a second and then placed them on the table. June got up from her chair and started walking towards the backdoor. She passed through the crowd, reporters, and the rest of the press. She could hear the confused voices of people wondering where she was going. As she was walking, the girl opened the back door and walked out. June started walking faster to catch up to her. When June was outside, she closed the door to the event and then locked it. The back parking lot was empty in her view except for the girl leading up to the event door.

The girl had short black hair, thin eyebrows, and brown skin. Her outfit consisted of red and yellow. "I got your attention." Before June could respond, they said with in low voice, "I don't think you need questions; you need answers," with crossed arms. "What do you mean?" June asked. "In 1995, I worked for the exhibit," they said. June's eyes widened as she listened to her speech about their experience. "The owner wouldn't let me enter my paintings," they said while frowning. "We didn't get along, so when the painting was stolen, they blamed me for accepting the painting for the exhibit," she said while now standing across from June. June rubbed the back of her head, trying to process the fact that she wasn't the only one framed. The person who would claim to have been tricked was Solari Cross, the person June is now talking to about the exhibit theft. "My name's Solari Cross," she said with an extended hand and a smile.

"I work for the tattoo shop a couple minutes from here; I thought I would stop by," she said while shaking June's hand. The framed art critic was looking down at Cross's hand, still processing everything she said. June asked, "Do you want to talk about this over dinner at my place?" Solari Cross agreed to dinner at June's apartment to talk about the situation. June realized that she had just walked out on all the reporters. "I should probably go back in," June said while opening the door back into the event center. When she opened the door, the crowd was silent. She broke the tension by making a joke about having to go to the bathroom. The crowd laughed at the fact that the event center didn't have any bathrooms.

The same day, Solari and June talked over the exhibit of Chinese takeout for dinner. " And then I thought, What's the second-best option for art?" Solari said this while sitting across from June in the bedroom of June's apartment. June took a bite of her chicken before saying, "Singing? Dancing?". Solari shook her head while turning on the TV. "No, a tattoo artist," she said while showing off her arm tattoo. "Do you want to see my back tattoo?" she added, trying to pull up her shirt. June stopped her with her hand before she got any further into the act. "No, I'll be okay," she said while smiling, her mouth full of chicken. Solari slept over in June's living room pullout bed since it was getting dark. The next morning, she thanked June for listening to her about the exhibit. "I'll see you whenever," she laughed as she walked out of the apartment. June waved at her from the door and then closed it. She fell to the ground and sighed while looking at a newspaper Solari had given her. She pointed at a face on the newspaper and then said, "Eddison Blackburn, a heist Lord."

8

Heists not just blackbirds - chapter 8

"I knew him really well," a fair-skinned woman with black hair said as she smoked her cigar outside of her house while talking to a reporter. "Do you know your husband is getting out of jail today?" the reporter said, flashing the camera in her face. The lady covered the camera with her hand and said, "That's none of your business." The audio cut off her voice because of the stormy weather. "We should really get going," the reporter from the van said. The lady watched as the reporter walked onto her porch. "Stop coming here!" she screamed as they drove away. Her name was Fannanah Andersen, and her husband was getting out of prison today. She put out her cigarette and said, "I'd rather have him rot in prison, anyway."

Fannanah's ex-husband, Lee, was bailed out of prison by an unknown person. "I don't know who let you out, but good luck," the police officer said as he walked him towards the car that would be taking him to the house he would be staying at. Lee didn't have anywhere to go because his family didn't even know he was alive, Fannanah hated him, and his old partners didn't trust him. When he got settled into the house, he dusted off an old phone book he found in one of the drawers. He pulled out one of the wall phones and called one of the numbers. "Hello, I know it's been 20 years; I wanted to call-" he said into the phone before they hung up on him.

Lee would have been celebrating retirement if he hadn't done the things he did. 20 years ago, he was sent to prison for completing a heist and second-degree murder that he wasn't guilty of. He sat on the sofa in the living room and turned on the television. He was surprised to see that one of the biggest news stories was a heist. It was all based around a woman that he felt didn't seem like someone who would steal something.

Lee completed five heists without being caught. He trained many people who would go on to become some of the deadliest criminals of their time. In his mind, he could sense that June was not the main person behind the heist. The heist seemed too simple for her to complete. He turned the channel to one to see a soup opera playing. As he was putting his feet on the sofa, his ankle bracelet unlocked and popped off. He jumped and fell over the back of the sofa. Lee was now on the hardwood floor, rubbing his back. He got up from the floor and started walking up the stairs. He was going to go to bed, forgetting that his ankle bracelet came off, until he heard a knock on the door.

9

Pale envelope - chapter 9

"Hello??" the older man yelled as he opened the door. He looked down to see a white envelope on the doorstep. He bent down to pick it up from the floor. He went back into the house and closed the door behind him. He looked down and thought about why they didn't put it in the mailbox to be picked up in the morning. It must have been really important to have been sent in at this time.

Lee ripped open the envelope from the top flap slightly. He saw a brown-papered letter inside, so he pulled it out. He sat down on the sofa and then began to read the letter. A couple of miles away, Solari Cross was closing up the tattoo shop she worked at. As she was closing up, she was on the phone with her boss. "Yes, he got his fifth tattoo today and gave me a tip," she laughed as she spoke about one of their regular customers. "Then she asked me on a date," she said while locking the shop up. She added, "I said yes; he seems like a good guy". As she was walking away from the shop, her boss started breaking up, so she hung up. She was walking into her car until she realized that it was too quiet. Solari could sense someone was watching her from behind; her back began to shiver. She pulled out a pocketknife and turned around to see a man standing in front of her.

Before she could open her mouth to scream, the shadowy man covered her mouth. Her muffled voice said "Get off of me", She was using her hands to get his hand off her mouth. He was using his other hand to hand her a white envelope. After that, he let go of her and started walking away. Solari couldn't see the man walk away, as her heart was still pacing. She looked down to see the envelope in her left hand. She scrambled up from the parking lot floor and started fast walking to her car. She unlocked her car with her keys, and she jumped into the car. She realized that she was still alive and thought about why he had just handed her the envelope. With both her hands on her car wheel, she looked down at the envelope that was now on the passenger seat.

At the exact same time she was being held up by the mysterious man, Caddock House was taking autographs from his fans at a bar he was at. He decided to leave early, as he didn't want to cause any conversation after his announcement of taking a break. As he walked out of the bar in an unbuttoned suit, he heard muffled screaming. His car was parked near the bar, but he was unsure where the noise was coming from. He looked into the space of the alleyway that connected to a parking lot. He saw a short-haired black lady being held up by a man with a white envelope in her hand. He saw him drop her off with the envelope. Then the man started rushing towards him, so he turned around to walk back to the bar. Until another man bumped into him. "Woah, I don't want any trouble," Caddock said, putting his hands up. The man didn't say a word, but he handed him a similar envelope that Solari was given. "What is this, the *Avengers* ceremony?" he chuckled before looking up to see the men had disappeared before his eyes.

June Flamingo unfolded the letter on her bed. She received it a couple of minutes ago at her door. She sighed before reading,

Dear June Flamingo

I have been watching you for a while. I feel your pain and your struggles. This is not your fault; I believe in you. I understand you; you had to lose your parents. Now your career is on the line.

Please come to this warehouse located in Clark County, Nevada.

I would like to form a team to get that painting back. I have located other people who are similarly connected with the thief, Eddison Blackburn. With skills that are all so different.

I will not be joining this team because I want to keep my identity secret. But I think this would be for the best. If you are to get the painting back, you will receive 1,000,000 dollars for whatever you want. I will receive the painting.

It was my brothers', so I feel like I should get it, but you will get your revenge, my darling.

From,

Artasque

June looked up from the envelope to meet face-to-face with her black television screen. She was thinking of all the possibilities of her getting kidnapped, murdered, or sent to a cult. But she also thought of some of the words that stood out. She was about to get up from the sofa until something really stood out to her: "Artasque".

10

Stranger Danger - chapter 10

The next morning, June got up and brushed her back in the mirror. Then she put her hair into a ponytail. Afterwards, she threw on the blue zip-up leather jacket and khakis. Then put on your regular sneakers. She ran out her door and into the elevator. She looked at her watch; the time was 10 a.m. It would take her about an hour to get to the warehouse, but it was enough time for her to think about who her partners would be.

The traffic was at its worst for a Sunday morning. June decided it was best to turn around and take a taxi. She huffed while sitting in traffic. June considered turning around and waving over a taxi driver. By the time she got there, she spotted a taxi driver parked near her apartment building. He was wearing a tuxedo and was leading the yellow taxi car. The sky was clear, and the sun was bright, so June would choose to put on her sunglasses.

He smirked at her while opening the back door. "*Mr. Cab Driver*, this isn't a date." "Besides, aren't you married?" *she* said while going into the backseat. He jumped into the driver's seat and said, "We aren't together anymore." She removed her sunglasses and said, "Don't try to flirt with me, and I'll call you whenever I need a taxi." He smiled before pulling out of the apartment. "A deal is a deal, Bird Lady." The ride was faster than she thought it would be because he took a shortcut to the warehouse. Before, she knew it was 1:00 p.m. and she was looking at a big warehouse in the middle of nowhere. She opened the backdoor because it was already unlocked.

"Listen, I was wearing the tux because I have a date this afternoon," he said while getting out of the taxi. June turned around before saying, "I understand; don't keep them waiting," as she waved him off.

June walked up to the giant warehouse with no door to open. So it was free for her to explore. The warehouse was covered with brown wood from the floor to the walls. It looked like an old building that was abandoned during construction. She saw big squares in the walls that made way for light to reflect off the wood floor. The warehouse was completely silent, with nothing but the wind to be heard. June took off her leather blue jacket to reveal a black tank top. She realized that she hadn't picked the best outfit for this meeting.

Valeria Woods was already sitting on one of the wood counters that were already set up. "Oh look, isn't it a Las Vegas criminal?" Valeria said, grabbing June's attention as she stopped in front of an entrance. June walked into the entrance with her coat to find out where the teenage girl's voice came from. She turned her head to find Valeria swinging her feet and hitting them onto the counters. "And who are you?" June said to Valeria with a confused look. Valeria replied, "Who are you, actually?" "Wait, don't answer that question." Valeria paused before adding, "I know you from the police station my father worked at." "You're one of his." June interrupted Valeria by saying, "That's none of your business." Valeria looked down for a second.

"I'm here because I got a letter from someone," June said while putting her hands into her jacket pockets to find it. Valeria explained that she had been here since that morning because of the letter. "Do you have it with you?" June asked. Valeria starts sweating a little bit before saying, "I left it at home." June didn't seem to question it, so Valeria sighed. "Wouldn't it be weird for you to get a painting you stole?" Valeria said jokingly to June. Valeria wanted to see how far June's strings could be pulled. June gasped in response. "Aren't you supposed to be at school?" she said, not answering her question. Valeria immediately replied, "Aren't you supposed to be in jail?" with the brightest smile she could muster. Before June could speak, both of them heard someone yelling behind her. A woman with short black hair wearing a comic-printed tank top and a jean skirt was walking towards them, waving her hands.

"Fight! Fight! Fight!" Solari began chanting almost in June's ears. Valeria began covering her ears before saying, "Girl, we are right here." June added, "We aren't going to fight, and I'm not going to jail for child abuse." June knew she had one of the first arguments with the future team, as Valeria didn't look pleased. Valeria jumped from the counters, suddenly matching the height of the other women in the room. "Aw, I wanted the first fight on this team." Solari laughed jokingly to June. The reason that Solari entered with so much joy was because most of the joy was rooted in the idea that she was finally going to get back at Eddison. They were all going to get back to Madison.

The three of them talked for a few minutes about the letter's details. The questions ranged from why the handwriting was so neat to who the mysterious person was. Solari said, "Wait, are we going to be an all-female heist team?" Solari added, "Like an ocean's 11, but all women," while putting her hands on June's shoulders. June looked at Solari while muttering, "I'm sure that's happened before." At that exact moment, they heard another voice behind them say, "Not quite, all female." The retired pro wrestler, Caddock House, was walking towards them. Before he could introduce himself, a gleeful teenager exclaimed, "You were in the wrestling match I went to." Caddock stopped in his spot before asking, "Which one?" Valeria replied, "The one where you lost. One of my co-workers took me." House's smile dropped as he heard the words "lost" come from Valeria's mouth.

"Congratulations, I guess." Solari slowly clapped her hands. June put her hands on top of Solarium's hands to stop her motions and then shook her head. "So, is this everyone?" June asked the room filled with strangers and a random person she just met a week ago.

"I cannot believe it." "This is all they could get," said an older man who came from the hallway in the warehouse that went to where the group was. "I'm sorry. Who are you? "I'm being serious this time," June said with her hands crossed. "Someone who just got out of jail for committing a heist," Lee said, coming to meet eye to eye with June. "Before you ask, I got the letter," he added. Solari was confused about whether he was saying that he was joining. With Lee's skills, they would have a fair chance against Eddison's team. "So you're doing it?" Solari chimed in while standing next to Valeria. Lee looked at Solari while replying, "No, I'm not going to do it." Lee rubbed his face and then added, "I don't think any of you should do it either, June specifically." Before Valeria was about to start walking out, she almost felt an earthquake. The only problem was that it wasn't an earthquake. It was a person, and it was June Flamingo.

"WHAT?!" the infamous art critic yelled.

11

Cold Pizza - Chapter 11

"We will be waiting in the other area," Caddock said, being the oldest of the three others not in the argument, motioning the girls to follow him. The only people in the room now were Lee and June. On one side stood a retired criminal who had just gotten out of his twenty-year sentence, divorced his wife, and lost all access to seeing his kids. On the other side stood the former art critic, who was framed, lost her parents in a homicide, and doesn't have kids.

"What do you mean, I can't do it?" June yelled at Lee. Her voice echoed through the walls of the warehouse as she put emphasis on her "I." "I have personally worked with Eddison," Lee replied, trying to reason with June. "He is a part-time thief and a full-time murderer," Lee said at the same voice level that June had just had. "I'm not scared of him," June said, not fully honest, as she knew deep inside she was. Eddison had ruined her life in the span of one day, and she had every right to be scared of him. "You should be; he doesn't just murder." "He gets people to murder," Eddison said, whispering towards June. June didn't say anything for a moment as her jaw clenched, thinking of Lee's words. "What if he finds out you're going after him like this?" "He will murder you himself!" Lee yelled, trying to get his point across. "There is nothing you can do," Lee finally said, waiting for June's response. June crossed her arms before repeating what he said. She said, "You're right, there's nothing I can do," while staring angrily into his eyes. She walked past him, brushing her arm against his. He stood there, realizing that he might have crossed the line.

The group decided to spend the night at the warehouse. Solari drove out to get pizza from the nearest area. "Forgive me for being late," Solari said dramatically. She dropped the pizza on the table that she had also brought back from her apartment. "We should give this place a makeover," Valeria said, opening the pizza box to grab a slice of pizza. "How about we eat this before it gets cold?" Caddock said as he realized that it was already freezing that night. Lee was standing near the wall, thinking about the argument from earlier. "Hey buddy, your pizza is getting cold," Caddock said, waving Lee over. Caddock realized that June was still outside on the small stairs that lead to the door of the warehouse. Solari nodded to Caddock as if she could read his mind. "Go talk to her. She's not mad at you." Solari said to Lee in an honest tone. "She's just really troubled, that's all," Solari added while preparing to take a bite of her pizza.

Lee acknowledged Solari's words and went outside to see June sitting on the edge of the stairs. Lee walked over to sit next to June. "About Earlier," Lee said before being cut off by June. "No need for apologies; Solari's right." "I wasn't mad at you," June said sadly to him. "It's not all about Blackburn," June sighed, trying to hold back tears. "I was raised in a foster home, and no one told me what happened to my parents," she said, looking at the empty road in front of them. "They never told me who did it; they said it was nothing I should worry about," she explained.

Lee listened to June explain her situation: wanting to protect her parents for so long. He realized that Eddison probably knew her parents' history. He used that against her. "Why did you change your last name?" Lee said this while looking at June. June looked down before saying, "I got a letter from someone in the mail, telling me to change it. I thought it was a threat," Lee sighed before rising from the stairs. He put his hand out to help June up. "What, so you're doing it?" June said, forcing a smile as she was still holding back tears. "Do one thing for me," Lee said, grabbing June's hand to help her up. June didn't respond because she was confused about what he was asking of her.

"Let me call you June Flamino," Lee said, meeting eye to eye with June. June gasped for a second, wondering why he would ask her such a question after he told her about the situation. "I'll repeat myself, Flamino," Lee said with a sly smile. "You'll do it if I let you use my last name." June said, standing in front of the entrance. Valeria was looking through the windows to see them standing in front. June could see Lee nodding, and she had no problem with it. "Yes, you can," June said. "Well, Flamino, the cold pizza awaits us," he said while grabbing June's hand. The group that was inside cheered once they realized that Lee was now on the team. The team was now formed, and Eddison was now about to meet his match.

12

Ready or not - chapter 12

It was a Friday afternoon in the year 2000 when the team decided to meet up again to discuss the letter but, mostly to discuss the roles they would be playing in this mission. Once everyone had made it, they set up one table in an empty area in the warehouse. The table was rectangle-shaped and gray-colored. To go with the table were five singular fold-out chairs. Solari was texting her boss on the phone, saying that she was taking a leave for a while in one of the chairs. Valeria was playing with her hands on the table and thinking about how she didn't have a letter to bring. Caddock was sitting to the left of Solari, looking up at the wall. Lee was leading up against the wall behind Caddock and Solari. June had been pacing around the room for about five minutes, reading over the letter.

Solari wanted to break the silence, so she said, "Isn't it exciting we could all be getting 1,000,000 dollars?" while putting her hands together. Valeria chimed in by saying, "This person must be rich." "Why does he need us?" Valeria was not being serious; she just wanted to add unneeded input. "Who cares why he needs us?" "We came here for a job," Caddock said to the blonde teenager sitting two seats away from him. June walked over to the table and placed the letter in front of them. "So we need a name!" she squealed with delight at the idea of having a cool name to represent them. "How about the frame?"

Valeria said she was looking directly at June.

June acted as if she didn't hear her as she picked up the paper to get a closer look. She pushed her brown, curly hair out of her face. "Who wrote the letter?" Suddenly, Lee spoke from behind Caddock. "I guess this is an Artasque person," June replied while pointing her hand at the paper with the signed signature. "Arta-sque," Valeria sounded out while folding her arms around her chest. "Arta-bay," Solari jokingly said after Valeria. Caddock looked at the two women sitting next to him, wondering if anyone had said it correctly. June put one of her hands on the table and thought about the name for a second. "Oh, June, you got something?" Solari asked.

"I like the name Artasque," June said while looking at everyone in the group. Solari and Valeria both looked at the retired criminal standing near June. The two of them were waiting for a response from him the most. "I like it." "It's so weird, it will get people talking," Lee said, nodding at June. The team then did a vote, and the name Artasque won. Caddock thought it was a good name because it made them stand out. Valeria thought it was a good name because the person who put them on this mission could find them easily. Solari just liked saying it, so she voted on it.

After picking their official heist team name, they decided on the roles of the group. Lee was in charge of assisting roles, mostly because June had no knowledge of how a heist actually works. Lee lined everyone up, including June, and went down the line for the roles. He decided that in the next few weeks, he would train them individually. "So, you want to do a heist?" Lee said while holding out a clipboard. On the clipboard was a white sheet of paper with everyone's full names written. "I think it's more of a reverse heist," Valeria challenged, causing Lee to stop moving. "Not the time," Solari whispered to Valeria, whom she placed next to.

Lee heard Valeria and realized that she was the first person with whom he was going to assist. He turned around to walk back to where Valeria was standing.

Valeria regretted her choice of words as soon as she saw him standing in front of her. "You're actually right; good job," Lee said while resuming walking back and forth in front of them. Valeria put her hand on her heart to inhale the air. "Do you have any relations with Eddison Blackburn?" he asked Valeria while holding his clipboard firm. Valeria answered, "No, I don't work with criminals." "Until now," she would regret her words again.

"Why did you ask?" Valeria asked, thinking he was purposely putting her on the spot. Lee mentioned that Caddock used to be in Blackburn's personal fight club before he was famous. Blackburn bought one of Solari's paintings when she was a small artist. "And you know June's situation," he said, while giving June a small smirk. He wrote something in a black pen on the clipboard. "So you're kicking me off?" Valeria yelled from her spot in the line. Solari was shocked, since this was the first time she heard Valeria yell. "Kid, I'm not." "You're the wildcard," he said while writing on the clipboard paper.

Valeria didn't say a word while he was assisting everyone else in their roles. She thought she was about to be put through the worst training of her life and then put to the side. But really, everyone had big parts in this heist, and Valeria had one of the most important roles. Solari was assisted the hacker role since she had told him that morning that she hacked into computers when she was in high school. "It was a prank," Solari said to Lee that morning. Lee nodded his head in response. Caddock was automatically assisted by "the muscle", and since he was older, Lee knew he would be much help in that department. That left June's role on the team.

"So, who's the leader?" Solari said, breaking the silence. Both Lee and June stared at each other. "Do we need a leader?" Valeria said this while folding her arms. The wind from outside was making it chilly inside. "Okay, girls, let's go," Caddock said while walking, almost touching Solari's arm. Before, Lee put his hand up, understanding why he was leaving. "We are all adults here," Lee chuckled while writing something down on his clipboard. June didn't understand his sense of humor, and she knew where this was going.

She said, "What's so funny?" to Lee while everyone else remained silent.

June pointed out that he had not announced the leader yet. "I am," Lee said while continuing to write on his paper. Caddock was about to start walking to the room behind them, but Solari grabbed his arm. "And June's the conman." "Alright, see you all tomorrow," Lee said while putting his pen on a clipboard. As he was walking towards the front door of the warehouse, he shouted, "Training starts tomorrow." June felt like for a second she blocked too long, and everyone was already walking away. June ran after Lee to catch up to him. "So I'm a conman." "That's all you give me," June said to Lee while walking with him. She tried to keep up with his pace.

Lee came to a halt next to her, almost making her fall to the ground. He walked in front of her to meet her eyes. "I knew you wouldn't like it." "But you're a perfect conman," Lee said. Lee showed June his markings near his name. He explained that Eddison was the one who was scared of her. She was perfect for the role because she was able to fake being a good art critic for the rest of her life. "Gee, thanks. Should I be honored?" June said while shrugging her shoulders. "Better yet, be grateful," Lee said quickly before continuing to walk forward. He started chuckling once she realized that June was still standing.

"Okay, I'm playing." "But at least you're not the leader," Lee said, smiling at June, who wasn't smiling at him. June put her figure to his chest and said, "First of all, I'm the reason we're here." Lee, being 2 inches taller than June, said, "Blackburn would have still stolen that painting without framing you." June removed her figure with a quiet gasp. Lee looked around to see if the others were still there. He whispered, "Remember that blue leather jacket?" June looked at him with confusion. "The one I wore, why?" she said, wondering why he was whispering. "And you wore that to the meeting," he said, while turning around to walk slowly out the door. He added, "I don't know; I just can tell you've never done this before."

June stood there shocked, as she didn't have a comeback for that. But she knew that this was going to be a wild ride. "Why do you and Valeria hate me so much?" she shouted from the middle of the room, where she was still standing. June realized that he had already made it to his car, but she knew the answer to the question. The two people she mentioned did not hate her; they only admired her. They wanted her to really seek revenge against Blackburn, but they didn't know if she could. The truth is, she could, and she was about to seek more than revenge.

13

Flamed store - chapter 13

The reverse heist team would meet for the next few weeks. The first week would consist of the training of Valeria, Caddock, Solari, and June. The second week would consist of them getting ready for the main event: the heist. Once they got a white board to place in the warehouse, they started planning out the directions for the heist. All the members had personalized training run by Lee himself. The first meeting would be with Solari. "So do I get cool glasses, or is that–" Solari began saying before Lee put one figure up. The two of them were in his car, driving to an abandoned store at a stop sign in the middle of Nevada. Lee's training wasn't really training; he just wanted to see what they could do with their skills.

Once they arrived in the empty parking lot, he parked off to the side. Then he pulled out a foldable table, a computer, and a chair. Solari put her hands in her coat pocket as she followed him to the store. The two of them were in front, but at each end of the parking lot. "Do what you can with the store," Lee said while leaving the computer for Solari. A few hours earlier, before picking her up, he had pulled a few wires into the store. The team was definitely never meant to be perfect, but he just wanted to see Eddison pay to put him in jail. For a few minutes, Solari would play with the key codes on the computer. Lee stood behind Solari, almost bending down to see what she was doing. She put her hand up, almost hitting him in the face.

An hour had passed, and nothing happened. Lee rubbed his beard, wondering what was going on with Solari's head. Until they both heard a cracking sound come from near the store. The wires broke, the windows shattered, and the roof fire alarm went off. The whole store went up in flames. Solari jumped up from her seat and put her hands up in happiness. "I can't believe this," she said while turning to Lee. Lee was too busy being blinded by a free fireworks show.

"So she set the store on fire," Valeria said while standing in front of a fake security detector. Lee nodded with coal still in his hair because the store ended up exploding while they were near it. He decided to end Solari's session early and start Valeria's early. "Before you ask, I am flexible," she said while wearing workout attire. Lee responded, "Why would I ask you that?" Lee realized that he had assumed that since she was the youngest, she would be doing all the things that require flexibility. "In elementary school, I was flipping in midair," Valeria said while stretching her arms.

She jumped up two times before running towards the structure that Lee had built to test her. Before Lee could stop her, she had completed it. He put a check mark near her name and put a thumbs up that she saw from the other side. Caddock didn't have much training, but Lee did explain what his role would be. June and Caddock's sessions would end up being combined. "I will do my best to protect her," Caddock said while standing across from June and Lee. "Oh, my hero," she joked while waving her hands like she was royalty. "I think we should really start planning the heist," June insisted while tapping her feet once. Caddock and Lee both looked at each other. "What? I'm the bait already," June said, while turning to look at both of them. Lee responded directly to June, "Punch me, and I'll tell you."

June walked up to him and punched him in the gut. Lee didn't see it coming until he felt a stink in his chest. He put his hand on his stomach and said, "I should really stop playing with you." June smiled as she playfully asked Caddock to walk her out as she was a princess.

Lee explained that Eddison was going to throw his annual ball in two weeks. "We need to find a way to get into one of his bases," Lee said to the team. "And get the directions," Valeria added questionably. "And get caught!" June said while sitting down and looking at Lee's notes. Everyone on the team looked at her as she questioned the leader's plan. "What if we weren't so direct in stealing the directions?" June asked Lee. "What if we made an appearance at this ball?" she added questionably. Solari smiled at June before chiming in. "What if we made the public know about us?" Lee looked at his notes on the board, and then he erased them. "Artaque is making a public appearance, and then we are taking the painting," Lee said to everyone. Caddock was silent for a while until he said, "So how are we getting the directions?"

Lee came up with a new plan involving two of the members distracting the security cameras in front of Blackburn's team's secret base. Then Caddock and he would sneak into the base and grab the directions from one of the computers. Then they would put it on a drive. Solari thought that it would be too dangerous for them to show up by themselves. "We need something so weird," Solari said while waving one of her hands. "So Artasque?" Valeria questioned. The whole team laughed at the idea of something being "So Artasque." But, really, the idea she was about to say was about to fit for this team. No other team has pulled something like this.

"I need something from one of my fashion friends," Solari said while getting up. She asked everyone to come with her in her car. The whole team ended up driving all the way to Solari's old friend, who owned a thrift shop. The whole team walked in, as Solari insisted. A tanned older lady with curly red hair walked out from the back of the desk. "What is this, babysitting?" the lady laughed. None of the team members thought the joke was funny. June was just happy she didn't make a criminal joke, as she was standing next to a real one. She watched as Solari spoke to the lady, and their heads shook as they spoke. Something from the lady caught her attention: "You need my mannequins?"

14

Mannequin business - chapter 14

Solari's plan was that she and one of the other girls were going to pretend to be entertainers in front of the cameras at the casinos. The casino was known to be one of the Eddison's team meetup places. While they found a way to get into the team meet-up place, whoever was left would watch the front. From inside, the girls would get directions for the ball. The stylist, Solari, was asking mannequins to help her parents with their event outfits.

"No, I'm not letting you take them," the stylist said while walking back to her office. Solari followed them painstakingly, repeating multiple pleas. "You sound like your father." "The answer's still no," the lady said while fixing her fur coat.

Solari frowned. "I'll give you money," she said while pulling out crumpled dollars from her back pocket. The stylist pushed the money away from her as Solari tried to hand it in. Solari put the money back into her pocket, realizing that she had no choice but to expose the mission. The lady reapplied her makeup from her small mirror and sighed as she realized Solari was still standing there. "I have serious customers coming in; say what you've got to say," the lady complained while whipping her hair back. Solari grabbed the lady's hand and pulled her to the curtain that acted as a door for her office. Solari pulled the curtain back to show a view of the rest of the team standing outside the shop.

"You see that woman right there? That's June Flamingo." Solari said she pointed towards June, who was talking to Lee at the moment. The lady had the urge to respond with a lot of fuss about her pulling on her expensive coat, but she knew the drama that was attached to June's name. The lady stepped back and sighed. "Fine, What do you want?" Solari squealed with excitement, and then she asked the lady for a piece of paper to show them the looks they would like to have made. Solari had previous skills as a tattoo artist. But she wasn't skilled at making clothing sketches.

Solari put a pencil to the paper on the stylist's desk. Solari scribbled and then erased again. She was thinking of something that could also keep their identities a secret. After thirty minutes, Solari had finished one singular sketch. She stood up and handed her sketch to the stylist, who had just come back with coffee. The stylist grabbed the sketch from Solari's hand and placed her coffee cup down. The stylist put on her glasses that were previously been on her head and stared at the sketch. "Are you sure?" The stylist said she was scrunching her face. Solari nodded at the question.

The stylist told her that this wouldn't take her too long, as it wasn't too much to do. Solari walked out of their office and into their space. When she walked outside, she told the team that the design had been accepted and that it would only take her two hours to make it.

She realized that Lee had left. "He saw people whispering, so he went home," Valeria said boredly while sitting on the edge of the window. June and Caddock had left for lunch, and Valeria decided to stay behind to wait for Solari. "The rest are at the diner across the street; I'm not that hungry," Valeria added. It was in the middle of the day when they were eating, so it wasn't as busy. When they were walking up, Caddock was talking to June about his wrestling training. They waved Valeria and Solari over. June was cutting a steak that she had ordered, and Caddock was about to take a bite into his hamburger.

"I'm surprised you didn't leave with all the talk about you," Valeria said directly to June. June didn't respond for a second as she ate a piece of her steak. "Remember who the real criminal is," June said as she gave Valeria a fake smile.

The team couldn't talk about the mission in the diner since it was a public place. But they decided to talk about their lives. "What grades did you have in school, Valeria?" Caddock said while sitting next to her in the booth. Valeria responded, "I was home schooled; I don't really remember my grades." Solari said, "You must have been lonely." Valeria laughed, saying, "Trust me, I wasn't." The whole group laughed with Valeria, not knowing why she was laughing. One of the waiters noticed that Solari and Valeria didn't have food and went over to serve them. The waiter was a dark-skinned man who was tall.

"Hello, What can I get for you?" he began saying before seeing June sitting on the right side of the booth. Solari began reaching for the menu, as she hadn't thought of anything. She opened it to see the options and responded, "I would like the sub sandwich, please." "Hold the mayo." The waiter ignored Solari and said, "Ma'am, I'm going to have to ask you to leave." Caddock put his head down, knowing where this was going. "I just asked for a sub," Solari began before Valeria gave her a look while sitting across from her in the booth.

"Why?" June said that while finishing a bite of her steak, she seemed unbothered by the words of the waiter. "You're going to cause trouble for our customers," the waiter said while looking at another person standing behind the counter. "What trouble?" June said, while thinking this was a different waiter that served them. The other waiter may not have known about her conference from early that month. Caddock was sitting stiffly as he looked above the booth to see customers staring. He grabbed June's hand, which was now on the table, gently. "June, please, it is not worth it," he whispered. Valeria clenched her fist as she realized that June was getting kicked out for doing nothing. "Fine, if she goes." "We are going to!" Valeria yelled. Valeria motioned for Caddock to get up so they could go. June followed them out of the diner. Solari yelled, "Yeah, no one likes your sub sandwiches," as she moved out of the booth. The waiter stood there in shock that they actually left; they thought they would put up a fight. Which they wanted for the cameras, specifically from June. June walked out sadly as she thought about the reason she was kicked out. Valeria stopped to wait for June to catch up. Caddock and Valeria put their arms around June in a half-hug. "Lee is going to be so mad at us," Valeria said. June chuckled, "Well, we got a first appearance."

The next morning at the warehouse, Lee was holding a newspaper in his hands. The rest of the team were sitting at the table in the warehouse, except for Solari, who was picking up the finished outfits. "Sub sandwiches," he said while palming his face. "I mean, you should be happy Solari's the hacker," June jokes. Lee dropped the newspaper on the table and walked over to June. June started slumping in her chair when she realized that Lee was not happy. Lee sighed as he passed June to walk over to the board. "This is just the beginning," Lee said to the group. Solari rushed it with two hangers and two custom outfits. "It's crazy that this was free," Solari said. Caddock asked, "What?" "Did you bribe her?" Solari went into a giggling fit as everyone collectively sighed. "No, she had an affair with my dad," Solari laughed, not joking.

Solari relieved the outfits from their covers. The outfits were bodysuits that were two-toned. One side of the bodysuit was black, and the other was white. The outfits resembled cat women in a way, but the mask covered the whole face. With a hole ontop for the hair and heels to match. "Ha, now who's going to wear this?" June laughed at the look of the outfits. Everyone looked at June at the same time. "Huh? Is there a bug on my face?" June said this while crossing her arms in her seat. "To be honest, Valeria can't do it," Caddock said while sitting next to June. June looked at him wide-eyed. Lee chimed in, "He's right." "Those men would eat her up." Valeria sighed happily at the thought that she was too young to be baited. Solari smiled widely at June as they stared at each other. June waved her arms in the air and said, "Oh, you've got to be kidding me!"

15

Emerald Bride - chapter 15

The two chosen people of the team put on the bodysuits that were custom made for the side mission. "June, can you help me zip this up?" Solari said. June, who was already well dressed, walked to the next room to help her. June looked at Solari up and down to see her dressed in a two-toned bodysuit. "Omg, we are twins!" Solari squealed. June didn't say a word as she walked to the front to meet the others. In front of the warehouse, Lee was showing Caddock and Valeria the van that he had gotten. "I found this in a dumpster yard, and it still works," Lee said to them. The van came with the technology they needed for both of their side missions and the big heist. Valeria, Lee, and Caddock would sit in the van and wait for the girls to get the directions.

It felt like Valeria was being talked to death by Lee. She looked behind her to see June and Valeria walking out of the warehouse. Valeria put her hand over her mouth to prevent herself from laughing, only for her muffled laughs to escape. Solari was standing with her hands on her hips, and Valeria had her back bent slightly. June wasn't insecure about herself, but even though the outfit fit tight, she wasn't sure why this was needed. "I think you look great," Caddock said in a cheeky tone. "I forgot something." Solari said as she waddled over to her car, as she wasn't used to walking in heels. June stood straight as she walked to the van, making eye contact with Lee. Until she grabbed the handle of the car and said, "Did they have weird costumes in your old heist groups?" to Lee. He shrugged his shoulders in response. "I'm just happy it's not me," Valeria laughed.

Solari came back with a white foam mannequin. June looked back to see an identical being holding a light mannequin in her hand. The second part of the bait was to make them so weirded out by not only what they were wearing but also that they had a mannequin on the side. "Do you want us to dance with it or something?" June yelled as Solari walked up to them. Solari laughed, "Lighten up," as she padded June's shoulder. June gave her the worst death stare she could muster. "Okay, let's go before June punches you in the gut," Caddock said to Solari. The drive to the casino was quiet, and it was 8:00 p.m. by the time they got there. Lee shouted from the front, "Are you two ready?"

The girls responded back and then hopped out of the back of the van. Solari almost fell to the ground before June caught her with both of her hands. She helped her stand up straight. Solari grabbed the mannequin that was on the floor of the van. Valeria closed the back of the van as soon as you could. Then Lee drove the van off to park somewhere. It was the middle of the night in Las Vegas, so their looks were not the weirdest thing on the streets. The two of them went on the concrete and followed the street to get to the side of the casino where the camera would be. The two of them both had microphones in their bodysuits for them to communicate with the rest of the team. Two other girls were walking drunkenly on the left side of them and were unfazed as they walked past them. The bright lights from the casino walls shone on June's face, which was covered by the white mask. The loud noises from inside the casino of people winning and losing money, June spotted an alleyway with a dumpster that was completely empty. Solari waddled over to the alleyway, and June followed her. June was used to walking in heels. When Soleri found the camera and a door to the backroom, she sat down on the mannequin. "Okay, so just follow my moves," Solari said as she waved her hands at June. "Why do we need the mannequin again?" June said, giving Solari a confused look with just her eyes. She thought they could easily just walk into the casino, but it seemed Solari wanted to take a different route.

"Play the music," Solari said into her microphone on her chest. In the van, Valeria put on *"These Boots Are Made for Walkin'" by Nancy Sinatra.* Solari started shaking her hips to the tune after she placed the mannequin in between them. She turned to the side to point at June to copy her moves. The two of them waited for someone inside to notice them, but it was only until the song was over. The door opened, and a man in a fully black suit took them inside. June was nervous but followed Solari, who was already halfway through the door. "Follow me," the man said as he showed them to the meeting room.

When they got there, he told them to sit on the sofa. June turned her microphone on for the rest of the team to hear. When they got there, there was a packed room filled with Eddisons' team. Eddison was not there with them, but June thought this was a meeting that didn't require him. June sat stiffly, not wanting to get comfortable with them at all. "I found these dancers outside; how much money do you want?" the man asked them. June didn't allow Solari to answer that question. "Free service," June responded while giving the biggest smile she has in a while. June looked down until she saw a bright orange-haired man in a white-collared shirt and dress pants. He looked younger than the rest of them, but still around Solari's age. Solari asked the group of men, after not accepting a smoke from the guy next to her, "Any parties coming up?" The man across from her responded, "Oh, a charity ball is coming up at *Bellagio.*" He paused for a second before adding, "On the 20th of the month." Lee wrote down what he heard on a piece of paper in the van. Solari realized that they had what they needed. She looked over to June to see her mixed expression at one of the men that just walked in. Solari whispered to June, "We've got to go, girl." She grabbed her arm as June was spacing out. June shook her head for a second until she realized that Solari was talking to her. "Forgive us, but we have to leave," Solari said while getting up from her seat. June got up with her while the men questioned why they were leaving so soon.

When they walked into the hallway, June stopped Solari. June stared at Solari without saying a word. "You look like you've seen a ghost," Solari whispered.

June explained that they needed to go back for something. "What, did you leave a heel?" Solari asked June, June looked around repeatedly and leaned in to say, "We need to take someone with us." Solari looked at June, wondering if she was really the crazy one in the group. "Are you insane?" Solari asked June. She explained that they could tell him that they were offering something if they came with them and then knock him out. Before Solari could respond, June was already back in the room. Solari decided it was best to keep walking to the van. But before she did, she unzipped the top of her bodysuit to grab a permanent black marker to write something on the wall. She wrote the words "Artasque was here" in big words. Then she quickly put it back into her bodysuit and took off her heels to start running to the van.

In the meeting room, June had asked the orange-haired man to follow her into the bathroom. In the bathroom, she took her heel off and knocked him out with it. He got out easier than she thought. She struggled to drag him out of the bathroom just in time to see Solari jogging her way. Solari ran faster when she saw June dragging the man on the floor. "This is why you're a conman," Solari said. June wasn't saying a word as she placed him on the floor. The two of them lifted him to the floor, where his arms were around their backs. The two of them, barefoot, ran to the van, which was in front of the casino. Valeria was sitting in the backseat when she saw them running with him around them. "I can't believe what I'm seeing," Valeria said as she hurriedly opened the back of the van. It was pitch black, but the two of them were the most visible things on the street.

The girls had used the door they came from to get out. Solari and June threw the man onto the floor of the van. Then they jumped in before Valeria closed it. Both of them were out of breath from running down the hallways. While panting, Solari said, "I can't believe you kidnapped someone." Valeria looked shocked as she seemed to agree with her comment. "Who's idea was this?" June still didn't say a word as she tried to catch her breath. Caddock got up from his front seat as Lee pulled off, still not hearing anything from the front. The bodysuit microphones were dead by this time. Caddock, bending down, swore. "It wasn't me!" Solari screamed. Caddock got to the same level as the rest of the group in the back. He was at a loss for words when he found out this was June's idea. "Lee, I think you're going to need to see this!" He screamed. Since Lee was driving, Valeria offered to drive them back to the warehouse. "Where in the plan is this?" the older man yelled. June was holding on to the side of the van as it was shaking.

From the front, Valeria was learning how to drive a van. Until she looked in her side-view mirror to see four men running towards the van from the lights. The thing that caught the teenager's eye was that they had guns. "Guys, we are literally being shot at right now," Valeria yelled to the back. Valeria speeds up the van a couple more miles than before to try to lose them. Even though they were on foot, the guns could still be felt from the back doors. Valeria started crying out of fear of dying at the sound of guns hitting her back. "Just keep driving!" Lee screamed as he was in the back. Solari was panicking at the thought of going to jail for kidnapping. "At least he's asleep," Caddock said to calm everyone's nerves. Until the man's eyes shot open to see a few of the two women in identical two-toned bodysuits, an older man and a wrestler he was familiar with, he could only see a glimpse of Valeria's blonde hair from the front.

Before he could fight his way out, Caddock knocked him out with his fist. Caddock, panting, said, "June makes it easier for everyone." He removed his hand from the guy's face and added, "Who is this?" June came back to reality, where everyone was staring at her like a deer caught in headlights. June sighed, "I wish I knew." Lee went back to the front after the response and switched out with Valeria, who had tears on her face. Lee said to June from the front, "We are going to have a long night."

16

We are Dunned - chapter 16

When they got back to the warehouse, June and Solari changed back into their normal clothes. The rest of the team strapped the man onto a chair with a rope that was in the van. Then put a table in front of him. Nothing else was in this part of the warehouse but the chair and the table. "Wake him up," June said while walking towards where everyone else was. Solari was trying to stop June from doing anything she would regret later. Valeria screamed really loud in response. The man's eyes shot open from the sound to meet with the people he saw before he was hit. A woman wearing a red turtleneck and black pants stepped in front of him. "June, oh my," the man said while looking down to see he was strapped down. He started pleading for his life.

"Gee, "What did you do that got him like this?" Solari asked June, waving her hands up. Lee, Valeria, and Caddock didn't say a word. They decided it was best to let June handle this early. Until Valeria asked, "What is your name?" The man put his head up and said, "Alex Dunn." June clenched her fists and asked, "Do you remember what you did to me?" June scrunched her nose while leading over the table. "You ruined my career, why?" she screamed at him. "I never ruined your career; it wasn't me," Alex said. June muttered that he was a lair. "Okay, I was a part of it," Alex added. Valeria stood against the wall and asked, "What do you mean, you ruined her career?" June looked at Valeria and then back at Alex.

Alex sighed, knowing that he wouldn't make it out alive if he didn't tell the truth. "Five years ago, my boss and I stole the painting," Alex said. He frowned. "We used June as a distraction; I never thought people would really think she did it." Lee walked behind June, who was building up anger as Alex spoke. "Keep going," Lee told Alex. "I found the painting a few months before this," Alex said. Alex explained that the person who owned the painting had died in an apartment. But he never told Eddison when the painter had died. "I looked at the person who died a little more, to find out—" he paused while stuttering. He didn't know if he should finish his sentence.

It felt like the world had stopped before Alex finished the sentence. Valeria was listening to him tell the real truth, realizing that June never stole the painting. Solari was shocked that he would tell her these things, and Caddock was covering his face in worry. Lee was slowly getting ready to grab June's arms from her back. Alex looked directly into June's eyes before saying, "The painter who died was Stephen Flamino." "June, it was your father." It's like the world began to move again. "You're a liar!" June said as she reached across the table while Lee was holding her back. Alex put his head back to prevent being scratched by June's nails. She repeated her words multiple times as everyone else panicked at the thought that they were now getting to back June's father's painting. June looked up while leading on the table at Alex's emotionless face. She realized that she wasn't lying. She put her head on the table while tears came down her face. "What was the name of the painting?" June said, gasping for air. The whole room went silent as they waited for a response. Alex responded, "The Emerald Bride." June began wailing and crying for a long moment, and Lee let go of her. Lee walked over to Alex and said, "Don't ever speak of this moment" while untying his ropes. Lee drove Valeria and Solari to their homes. The time was 12 p.m., but Valeria told her parents she was hanging out with some friends.

A few minutes had passed, and June's face was on the wet table that was covered with her tears. Caddock was afraid that if he did anything, she would burst into flames. He imagined how it must feel to find out that she was really meant to live rich and that all of that was taken from her. "He never told me when they died," June said while her head was on the table. Caddock came to the side of the table and kneeled down to her level. "I think it's good that he didn't," Caddock said, patting June's back. It was because now June had another reason to prepare for the public meeting with Eddison at the ball. She wasn't going to get that painting back to cover her; she was going to get it back for revenge.

17

Fannanah - chapter 17

Over the next couple of days, the team would prepare for the annual ball at the hotel in Las Vegas. The side mission was that they were going to crash Eddison's party before the big heist. But the only problem was that they had no outfits. "I can't threaten that lady to expose her affair to her husband again; any ideas?" Solari asked the group. It was one of the hottest days, and everyone was holding fans in the warehouse. "I have fifty dollars on me," Valeria said while referencing the money she got from work. Her co-workers were probably worried about her, but she wasn't going back to that car wash job.

The suits would be the easiest of them all, so Lee had already stopped by a shop to buy two suits. But Solari suggested that the women have different looks to stand out. "Everyone's going to be wearing black," June said while sitting on the floor. Everyone looked at Lee, the alleged leader of the team. "I know a person," Lee said, not making eye contact with anyone. "She doesn't like visitors or me," Lee added. June laughed, "Time to bribe," as she pulled Lee's arm into his car. The rest of the group followed them. The team had decided on Lee's car for this. The person that they were going to be visiting would be someone he hadn't seen in a long time.

When they got to the brownish suburban house, Lee walked up to the front door. The rest of the team waited for him in the car. He looked back before slowly knocking on the door and walking up to the front door. The rest of the team waited for him in the car. He looked back before slowly knocking on the door. He was looking at the floor when a pale-faced lady with black hair opened it. She had rose lips and reddish circles around her eyes. He saw four teenagers on her back until they scrambled to the second floor. "Lee?" she questioned, sensing he looked older than he did twenty years ago. Once he realized it was him, she looked behind him to see Solari waving rapidly.

She invited the team in for lemonade, which was fitting because she was wearing a sundress. "This isn't how I wanted to see you again," Lee said while sitting down on the sofa in the living room. She was about to respond before Solari said, "You have kids at your age." The lady laughed and said, "I'm fifty, but thank you." June whispered something to Caddock and then looked at Lee. He was still shocked that his divorced wife still looked the same way he left her. Her skin looked white like snow and was soft to the touch. Until a man walked down the stairs with glasses on. "Hun, who are your friends?" the man said while giving the lady a kiss on the cheek. She was still holding a lemonade bottle in her hand. She introduced him to Lee, and they shook hands. Then he walked back upstairs to avoid any weirdness.

"I need three outfits from you; I have money," he said, pulling out one hundred-dollar bills. She laughed, "Hold on, what for?" June stood up and said, "I'm June Flamino." The team looked at her from the sofa. Valeria took a slow sip of her drink. "Oh, I'm sorry that was awkward." June stood tense for a moment. "Is this your ex?" she said while turning her head down to look at Lee. He nodded his head slowly. June explained what the mission was and why they needed the dresses while standing up. She agreed to help them. "Come on girls, I need measurements," she said while putting the lemonade in the kitchen. "By the way, my name's Fannanah," she said, while she reached out to shake June's hand.

Fannanah was known to work with hiesters because she was once working with Lee. She had to quit her career because Eddison's team was targeting her business. She was forced to take private orders. So she was honored to help them get back at Eddison in some way.

After she got measurements, she spoke to the girls individually about what they wanted for their looks. Then everyone left, as it would take her until the day after the ball for her to finish. Fannanah started working on Solari's dress first. She took note that Solari loved blue and didn't want a very tight dress. She decided on a turquoise dress skirt paired with a long, flowing train. The top of the dress would be covered in white jewels. Her tattooed arms and legs would be on display. The second dress was for Valeria. She noted that Valeria did not want to stand out too much. So she went for the colors that were chosen as the theme for the ball: black and white. She made a long dress with black and white stripes on the bottom and a black top piece.

Lastly, the dress that would stand out the most would be a corseted emerald dress with a long, flowing bottom piece. The dress would go to June, even though she didn't know what type of dress she wanted. The designer would work day and night to make sure they were done before the ball. Before she knew it, it was time to send them out to the team. It was time for the big revelation. Lee went by the house the day of the ball to get the dresses. Fannanah and Lee did not speak a word to each other. They only nodded at each other. When he put the dresses in the backseat of his car, he saw a letter on the top of the covers. The letter read:

Dear Lee,
  I'm happy that you're finding a way to twist this career of yours into something good.
  Even though we parted ways, just know your kids love you.
  They wish they could be with you. I hope once Eddison is gone.
  You can come see them or see me.
  From,
  Fannanah

Lee waved to Fannanah from his car seat. He had fallen out of love for her after she told the police what he was doing. He knew she was lying, so he could split anything he had got from Eddison with her. But he didn't want to see her right now. He was focused on helping someone he loved more at the moment. He would only go see his kids after this was over. He wouldn't be going to see her because she never wanted to see him.

<h1 style="text-align:center">18</h1>

Ball Crash - Chapter 18

The day finally came for the event. It was the 20th of June. The team met at the warehouse to get ready ten hours before the event would start. Lee brought the girls' dresses that he kept at his house until the day of. He decided to go over the plan before they headed out. "We will arrive in the van and then sneak out when it gets crowded at the entrance". The team was listening as everyone circled the table where they did the majority of the planning. "What if we get caught?" Valeria said this while crossing her arms. "I'm the youngest person on this team; if we get caught, I'll have no luck getting into college," she said to the group. Everyone turned to look at her.

June, who was handing Caddock a soda, said, "We are heisting in five days". Lee quickly turned to June, saying, "Actually, ten days". He explained that Eddison would think they were trying to get the painting back if something happened so close to the event. "Why five days more?" June asked Lee before taking a sip of her soda. "Never ask the mastermind questions," Solari laughed. Lee didn't answer June's question. June vended her eyebrow, giving Lee a look because he didn't answer her question. "Okay, review the plan," Caddock said to break the awkward silence. "Right, Solari and Valeria, enter first," he said, while pointing at a map with everyone's names connected on the table. "We need to get people staring at the entrance," Lee added. "June enters in afterwards?" Solari asked. Lee nodded while looking at the table. "Me and Caddock monitor Eddison," Lee said to the group. The team would be free to mingle around the event, but they could not cause any trouble. Lee never told them they couldn't cause any trouble.

After they went over the plan, they went to get dressed in separate areas. Caddock got dressed in the van so he could figure out the location. Everyone else stands in the warehouse. Solari was the first person to get into her dress. Valeria followed suit since her dress was easy to slip over her head. When they walked to the van, they bumped into each other. Solari was about to say something before Valeria stopped her by looking sideways to see June struggling to fix her corset. The dress was on, but the back ties were not tight. June shrugged for a second. "Are you just going to stand there?" she said. Solari and Valeria rushed over to help her tighten up the back of her dress. As Valeria and Solari grabbed both laces, June could feel her stomach clinch. She gasped for air and held on to the wall. "How tight can we go with this?" Valeria looked at Solari. As this was happening, Lee was walking past them in his tuxedo when he stopped to take a second glance. Solari makes eye contact with Lee. June looked to her side for a second until she realized it was Lee. "We don't have much time," Valeria added, gasping for air as she struggled to tighten the back. Lee walked over to Valeria and Solari. He motioned for them to move out of the way so he could tighten June's back on his own. He did it without ease. June almost fell to the ground as she gasped for air as the corset was tightened. Valeria was nervously laughing while June was angrily staring without looking at them.

Lee walked out of the room without saying a word. The girls helped June walk to the van as she was struggling to breathe. Once they got to the car, Caddock started driving off, as they only had four hours for the event to start. They needed to be one of the first people to enter, and it would take them two hours to get there. June sat on one of the seats in the back and crossed her arms. Valeria was sitting in the front with Caddock. Solari joined Lee and June in the back. "You—" Lee spoke to June while looking at her. June interrupted him, saying, "Don't talk to me". Solari froze at the sudden response from June. "I was going to say you're great," Lee said. June looked out of the window for a second and looked back at Lee. "You look great too," June said to Lee. He could see the nerves in June's face, which were now covered in makeup. Her hair was curled out around her shoulders.

He wondered why it took them so long to tighten up her corset. Until he looked down at her back to see a lump in the shape of a gun. She must have been trying to tighten it herself until she saw the girls looking at her. Where did she get the gun? Why did she have the gun? These were the questions that Lee asked himself. He didn't want to ask her about it now, with the mission on the line. But was it really his mission? Before he could try to speak to her, the van had come to a halt. Caddock had stopped the car in front of the hotel, where people would be greeting guests. Valeria had finished talking to him about her future career once she went to college. "So how are we getting in?" Valeria asked. Caddock looked at her and then chuckled to himself. This was the first time Valeria saw him laugh during any of the meetings. "Simple, with my old celebrity status," he said, while he rolled down the window to see an officer. The officer asked for an ID and realized that Caddock used to work for Eddison.

The officer opened the backdoor, which caused June to jump slightly. The officer asked for Solari's hand to help her out of the van. Another officer came over to help Valeria out. June seemed to be more anxious than normal. Lee touched June's exposed shoulder and whispered, "I can walk you out if you don't want anyone to find out". June didn't know at the time what he was talking about. She thought he was talking about her name, but he really was talking about the gun she smuggled in. Once they got into the event hallways, they were packed with all different types of people. June, who could tell who the really rich people were by how they dressed, She looked back to see Caddock speaking to one of the officers about the entrance. "I don't know if I can do that," the officer said to Caddock. "It's a surprise for Eddison," Caddock said while pulling out a fifty-dollar bill from his pocket. "Under one condition, you need to do it fast," the officer said loudly because the music from inside had started playing. Caddock rushed over to June; Solari had gotten distracted by one of the guys from the casino noticing her. Caddock grabbed Solari's arm so she could kiss him. "Not the time!" he yelled. Valeria quickly followed after them. Solari spoke loudly back at the guy while she was holding Caddock's hand, "We aren't together!".

The entrance was completely open, with curtains covering it slightly. June peeked inside for a second to see Eddison speaking with Alex with a wineglass in his hand. The two of them were near the stage, where the singer was getting ready to perform. Caddock whispered to the officer, and the officer walked inside. The officer grabbed a microphone from one of the stands on stage. The singer stood in shock, but also in confusion. "What's the meaning of this?" they said in a French accent. Eddison didn't say anything as he waited for the officer to speak. "Please welcome retired wrestler Caddock House," the officer said through the microphone. Caddock walked through the entrance and waved at the crowd that was standing in the hall. The crowd cheered, and others looked at each other, confused. Caddock heard whispers from the crowd. Lee would not be announced; instead, he would be watching June. After what he saw, for different reasons. The officer would not announce Valeria and Solari. But they did walk in together. The crowd was in awe as they showed off their custom-made dresses. Some of the girls gave devilish looks at the idea that these random people had better dresses than them. Also, Solari wasn't wearing black or white.

"Who are these people?" Alex whispered to Eddison. He put his drink up to be refilled. "I think the first one was in one of my old fight clubs, the girls I'm unsure," Eddison said. The officer coughed to himself. "Please welcome a special guest," he said into the microphone. Eddison's head shot up to see who it was. Everyone was standing on the sides of the hall, so there was a lot of room for June to walk in. She stepped in with both heels. She stood as she waited for the officer to say her name. "June Flamino," the officer said on the microphone before realizing the last name he had said. The crowd collectively gasped as they saw June stand. The gasps were because the dress resembled a specific person. The other gasps were because they didn't use her current name, Flamingo. Eddison spit his drink out; the wine was staining his suit. He looked down and up as June made eye contact with him. She gave him a sly smile, knowing she had got him.

Eddison felt embarrassed as the host of the party, so he left for the back area to get changed into a new shirt. His crew followed him. Alex stood frozen as he looked back at Lee, who was looking at him. He took a sip of his drink slowly. After a few minutes, Eddison returned. He gave out awards to his team and honored his colleague, Alex. Then it was time for the partnered dancing. June was finishing one of the dishes that one of the servers overcooked. June could not eat in her outfit, so put her cloth to her face to wipe her mouth. She looked around to find the rest of the team. Caddock was speaking to a group of his fans. Solari was enjoying a conversation with the guy she saw early. Valeria was feasting on the gourmet food. June couldn't find Lee; she hoped he had not forgotten that this was just a side mission. Eddison walked over to June, who looked up from her seat. "May I help you?" June asked as he stared. He fixed his suit before asking, "You look ravishing. May I dance with you?". She did a double take until she realized this was what she wanted. She offered him her hand as he guided her to the center of the floor.

June took her steps easily, as she wasn't good at ballroom dancing. She had never ballroom danced before. She decided just to follow his moves. Lee looked at June from the second floor of the hall as he looked directly at her hand movement. "You know we aren't so different," Eddison whispered as his face got closer to her ear. June's jaw clenched at his words. "I beg to differ," she whispered. "The last name?" Eddison said to June: She was down in a dip. "I didn't choose to use it," she said as he pulled her up. "The color green suits you," he whispered to June. Her eyes widened as she remembered what Alex said about her father's painting was. "It's just a color," she said, frowning a little as he called her again. When she was titled, she saw an upside-down Alex.

June realized that the reason they framed her was because Eddison knew about her old name. People thought she stole it to get back at her parents for being murdered. To get back at the world for throwing her into a foster home and never giving her a cent of her parents' money. That's why her father wanted her to change her name, because Eddison's team was after him. When her thoughts stopped, Eddison pulled her up. She grabbed the gun when his hand was covering hers. The whole crowd stared at them in the center. Lee looked down with his hands crossed. He mouthed something to Caddock from the top. Valeria stuffed her face before running back to the van. Solari was nowhere to be seen. Their faces were nose-length away; his hand was on her back; and the gun was in June's hand. She saw the same smile that he gave her that day. The day that everything changed, "Do it; send me to your father," he whispered. She clenched the gun in her hand that Fannanah had given her. "It's payback time, Flamino," he added.

She looked up over his head to see a blurry vision of Lee. She dropped the gun on the ground and ran. Lee ran down the stairs to try to catch up to her. Eddison covered the gun, so it wouldn't make a scene. Alex stood in shock at the sudden departure of June. "Please forgive me; my partner left," Eddison laughed. The crowd laughed with him, and the celebration went on. June ran as fast as she could until she tripped over her heels. "Guys, I can't find Solari!" Valeria yelled while picking up her dress. Solari came running towards Valeria and Caddock. Her lipstick was messy, and her hair was to the side. Valeria and Caddock looked at each other. Solari didn't say anything as they got in the van. Caddock waited for June and Lee. June got on both knees in her dress; she couldn't get up after that. Lee walked over and stood behind her. He didn't say a word until June said, "You knew, so why didn't you stop me?". Lee looked up at the sky. "A learning lesson," he laughed. She stiffened from the tears as she got off the concrete. "Are you mad at me?" she said as she walked with Lee. He laughed, "Not at all, sweetheart, not at all".

Vault Match - Chapter 19

It all started with a letter that was sent to a group of individuals. Valeria Woods is the teenager who was trying to get money to pay for her education while her parents kept secrets from her. Caddock House is the retired wrestler who never got along with his boss. Lee Anderson, the retired heisted, had just gotten out of jail for committing a huge heist with Eddison. Solari was an inspiring artist who wanted nothing more than to have her art shown in the biggest galleries. Lastly, June Flamingo, the hated art critic who had her reputation destroyed because she was framed by Eddison. Valeria fluffed her hair in a pocket mirror and then adjusted the collar of her white top. She had on jeans that she owned and a fake ID on her shirt. Solari came in behind her in her all-black outfit. The team expect for Valeria decided that they should all dress in black to not stand out. "Weird that we are all wearing black with a name that means art," Solari said before she laughed as she fixed her blazer.

"I know you're only in it for the money," Solari said out of the blue. Valeria froze with widened eyes as she stopped applying her makeup. "You're the only person on the team with no relations with Eddison," Solari said with a sly smile. Valeria put her pocket mirror in her back pockets and turned around to make eye contact with Solari. "You want the painting for yourself," Valeria blurted out. The rest of the team was getting ready in separate rooms. Caddock was starting up Solari's equipment. "You're jealous that June gets the praise for not even being an artist," Valeria said, looking up at Solari, who was currently wearing higher boots. "You want a piece of that, don't you?" Valeria asked her with a frown on her face. "June's not going to listen to you, of all people," Solari said with a sly smile look.

"Be quiet and enjoy the ride," Solari said while walking out. Valeria looked around, as if she wasn't innocent. She stood in the empty area and looked down. Then she walked out the same way that Solari did. June and Lee were talking to each other outside the warehouse. "Why did you actually say yes to doing this mission?" June asked Lee. He looked around and said, "Simply, I wanted to watch Eddison suffer." Lee looked at June. "Would you actually team up with Eddison?" he asked. June's eyes widened. "No! "Are you jealous?" she asked. Caddock could hear her laughing from inside the van. Lee stood speechless with an emotionless face. "I am not jealous!" he reassured. "Eddison's way better than me," he said, almost childlike. "Better yet," he said before June interrupted him by pulling him by his arms into a frantic kiss. Their lips came crashing together as Lee's eyes were still open for a second. He leaned into it as he grabbed hold of her waist, and her hands traveled to his neck. It almost felt like minutes before they pulled away from each other while breathing heavily. June tapped back into reality when Caddock turned the radio on, unaware of what they were doing. She removed her hands from his neck and said, "Um, that was a thank you for everything." "If Eddison shoots me," June said as she quickly made her way to the van. Lee stood there, and she looked to his side to see Valeria standing there. She had been standing there for minutes before realizing it.

When he got to the car, he sat next to Caddock to avoid the awkwardness. "How was the kiss?" Caddock asked. June and Lee both froze as he spoke. Caddock laughed and said, "No need to answer." The kiss was June's first since her early art critic days, but she never had a relationship. It was a one-night stand; she never had time to settle down. Solari and Valeria did not say a word to each other. Caddock put on the radio to calm everyone's nerves. The traffic was pretty calm for an early Friday morning, and the sun was bright. Once the team pulled up the newly painted white van, Caddock dropped off June and

Lee at the front of the mansion. June was wearing a wig to disguise herself; they would be looking for her.

"Let's not talk about it; we came here to do something." She spoke quietly to Lee as they walked to the side to wait for the doors to open. On the other hand, Caddock was switching seats with Solari. Once they got to the side, one of Eddison's cleaners opened the side door for them. The cleaner held the door open for Valeria as she held the empty box that would stand. Caddock followed after her. Valeria was holding the box stiffly. Caddock whispered to Valeria, "If you need me to open the vault, I can." Valeria shook her head quickly and said, "I'm fine; lead me to the vault." The two of them walked down the hallways while Caddock was holding a smaller version of a map that Lee had designed.

When Lee and June got in, they bent down to wait for the party guests to arrive. A person came up to them. "Are y'all extra servers?" they asked them. June and Lee would end up having to be servers to keep them inside the mansion. Solari was typing on the computer to see if she could get into the computers in the house. She thought that the passwords would probably be in there. After going through many passwords, she found a four-digit code: 3908. Solari told Caddock about the vault number and put the mic on his jacket. Valeria went towards the wall when she realized they were being followed. A man walked past them, and Valeria held her breath. Caddock joined her on the wall. "Keep going; I'll watch your back," he said. She nodded and took the paper from Caddock's hand. She followed her down a long hallway until she got to the vault. The vault was a big gray door, different colors from the tan wallpaper on the walls. Valeria looked back to see if anyone was there, and she carefully entered the code. The door opened, and she stuck inside. While this was all happening, one of Eddison's employees was telling Solari she couldn't sit in the van in the alley.

She moved the van to a back area and parked it. She decided to walk inside to sneak into one of the windows with a pick that she had. Solari already knew where the vault was and the code that was needed. She followed the empty trail as all the rest of the employees were preparing for the party. The time was three o'clock. Caddock saw Solari pass by him from the hallway next to him. He tried to get her attention, but she couldn't hear him. One of his employees came from the hallway instead. "You're coming with me," he said, grabbing Caddock's hand. With Caddock's wrestling skills, he knocked the employee to the ground by hitting him in the gut. The employee fell to the ground in pain, and Caddock ran to the vault. He called into his mic for Solari, but there was no answer. He ran as fast as he could, and in his vision, he saw Solari putting in the key code for the vault. His face went into the vault door, and he fell to the ground. He saw a blurry vision of Solari walking away. Valeria could see red lines following all over the place, and on the very edge of the painting stood a clear glass. She jumped over one of the red lines and almost lost her balance. Valeria stood on one foot, her hands in the air. She waited for one of the lines to pass, and then she put one foot down and slipped past the red line. Valeria was halfway through the security bars before she looked back to see Solari standing still. Her eyes widened as she began to lose balance.

While this was all happening, Caddock was trying to communicate with June and Lee. "Guys, I think Valeria's in trouble," he said as he struggled to get up from the floor. Lee looked at June, wondering what he could mean. Caddock got up on his feet and dusted himself off. Lee and June were currently in the coat closet of the party room kitchen. He hit the wall of the closet out of anger, and he walked outside. June tried to grab his hand and stop him from leaving. When Lee walked out, he ran into one of the servers. The server explained the meal plan that would be happening at the event. June popped out of the closet and waved from behind Lee. The two of them had to turn their microphones off so the servers wouldn't hear anything.

Caddock ran down the hallway into the vault and hid around the edge. He saw the back of Solari talking to Valeria. The blonde was struggling to hold her balance as Solari taunted her. "You're getting the money, anyway; why ruin this for us?" Valeria yelled back at Solari as she balanced on one foot. Solari decided the only way she was going to end this mission was if she set off the alarm. Solari's foot lifted from the ground within a moment. Before she could place it on the floor, Caddock wrapped his arms around her, bringing her back. The two of them dropped to the floor as he held her tightly. Valeria looked back as she was balancing to see Solari being held down. She panicked, and one of her feet hit one of the security lights. The sirens went off; the time was six o'clock. Solari laughed. "Shut up," Caddock said as he held her down. Valeria didn't look back as she ran to the glass that was open. She looked at Caddock and asked him to come help her take it down. Solari watched as Caddock let go of her and helped Valeria carefully lift the painting. The painting was lighter than they thought, and Solari stood still in her place. When they prepared to leave, Valeria looked shocked at the weight.

"Something is not right," Valeria told Caddock as he held the other side. "This isn't the real painting," she said as she shook her head. While this was all happening, Lee and June were helping set out plates for Eddison's evening party. The two of them had to find a way to get out of there before Eddison came. Lee walked to one of the hallways near the entrance to the grand hall and then turned on his microphone to hear screaming.

"I didn't take the painting," Solari screamed at Caddock. "You're on Eddison's side," he heard Valeria scream from the back. All the while, the sirens in the vault were going off. He looked at June, who was now standing in front of him, and they nodded. The two of them dropped their plates and ran to the vaults. Right past the front entrance, where Eddison was introducing himself to one of his newest guests. A security guard whispered to him that the vault alarm went off, and he smiled. He knew they were coming, so he hid the painting in a separate area.

"You really forgot what the painting looked like?" Valeria screamed at Caddock. all while holding the painting in the hallway inside the vault. June told Lee that she wanted to enter alone and that he should watch the vault doors. Eddison told his security to wait until later to welcome them. June walked down the short hallway to see Solari staring at Valeria, who was being held back by Caddock. Solari stopped as she saw June's shadow out of the corner of her eye and turned around. "Who sent you here?" June asked Solari in a low tone. Solari laughed evilly, saying, "I sent myself."

Solari was an inspiring painter who was working at the museum at the time when the real painting was stolen. Her employees blamed her for not noticing that the man was posing as an employee. Solari's boss ended up firing her for letting him sneak in. "I asked them for weeks to let me show my art; I was never getting a chance now," Solari explained. She never wanted revenge on Eddison; she only wanted revenge on the painting itself. "I was going to sell it privately," Solari said as she bent her eyebrows. June glared as she looked around her face to make eye contact with Valeria. "Yeah, Artasque offered me the job for the money." Valeria frowned as Caddock let go of her. She looked like she was saying "sorry" to June with her eyes.

June didn't know how she felt about finding out that two of her newest friends used her struggle to succeed. "If you excuse me, I'll be getting the real painting," Solari said as she was about to walk past June. Solari thought that she would either get the real painting or offer up June to the police by framing her for stealing it. June pulled out a gun and pointed at Solari's head. "I wish I knew," June said as she stared at Solari, emotionless, with the gun pointed to her forehead. "You sold me out; I'm going to jail if you take that painting," June said as she looked at her with her hand still pointed. Solari stood fearlessly with an evil eye on June. She knew she wasn't going to shoot her and risk going to jail for murder. June was about to pull the trigger before Lee came in from behind and pushed her into Solari. June rolled over to the side of Solari. Lee got up on his feet. "Get out of here!" he screamed at Caddock and Valeria. He knew that they had so much to lose if they stayed. June was in pain from being pushed at such speed.

She grumbled as she saw Solari get up from her feet to stand with Lee. Both of them looked down to see the gun filled with bullets on the ground. Solari grabbed it and shot Lee in the leg. The world froze, with only Solari moving within it. June gasped as she fell to her knees on the side of the now-wounded Lee. He held his leg against the stinging sensation of the bullet in it. "Don't do any of that lovey-dove stuff; I'll be fine," Lee said as he motioned for her to leave. "I'm not leaving you!" she yelled at Lee with a frown. "Besides, I'm getting arrested when I walk out of this mansion," she added. The blood dripped out of Lee's leg onto the floor, leaving a big puddle of blood that touched June's pants. June got up and tried to pull Lee around her shoulders to help him walk. She struggled to lift him with his weight, but he was able to hang his arm around her neck. Solari had only shot once into one of his legs.

June decided not to leave Lee because he would have bled out if he stayed; she wanted to be in jail knowing that her greatest friends have a good life. When she got into the hallway outside of the vault, she saw Caddock walking. He looked shocked at the blood stain covering Lee's leg and helped him onto his shoulder. June knew that Solari was probably already in the van. She breathed before beginning to walk to the entrance, and Lee whistled to get her attention. "Did I earn the leader's badge?" June asked while walking backwards. Lee smiled, and Caddock stopped to let him turn around. "You'll earn it if you get out," he yelled. The hallways were quiet as she slowly walked to the front entrance, accepting to be knocked down by officers.

The paintings filled the walls of Eddison's mansion hallways. She decided to stop in front of a familiar painting. The painting was giant and almost filled the walls. It was of a beautiful woman in an emerald dress who was sitting on a bench. The painting next to it was of someone who looked to be her mother. She thought about what Solari was talking about. Before she got turned around, and an officer wrapped handcuffs around her. June could not hear what he was saying; everything was blurry. The officer walked her outside to the entrance. The entrance gate was filled with expensive cars belonging to the guests. Some of the guests gossiped about each other; she knew they were talking about her. June looked down as she went into the police car; she didn't see Eddison standing near the police car. As she was in it, she saw Eddison shaking hands with one of the officers. Then he walked away and went back to his mansion. June stared at the backseat of the police car and thought about the rest of the team. About if they made it to the van safely or if Eddison wasn't planning on arresting them. She knew that Solari never got the painting in time, unless Eddison had copies of the painting to trick them. But all she knew was that Eddison would finally have proven that she tried to steal the painting.

20

Birds can fly - chapter 20

It was five days after the heist went wrong. I was spending most of my time in my cell, waiting to be judged by the jury. Most of the people in this prison were here for worse things than me. It's interesting to me that I would be in here for murder if it weren't for Lee. I find it interesting that I am now sitting in the same position he once was in prison for committing a huge heist. I felt the guilt run down my spine as I played with my fingers. I was wearing the normal orange jumpsuit, which was not comfortable.

I saw an officer standing at my cell, so I thought that it was time for lunch. So I bent down to the small slide that they had, but the officer told me that someone had bailed me out. With Eddison's power, he put my bail at 500,000. I wondered who could have bailed me out and how they had that much money. As I was walking out, the officer led me to where my clothes were. I had the same clothes I wore for the heist. I decided to wear the black turtleneck and the black jeans I had.

The officer led me to the entrance and opened the gate for me to walk out. The large parking lot was empty, with only one car sitting in it. The car was a blue Ferrari with shiny windows. I couldn't see who was in it, so I decided to take my chance. Before I could walk closer, the driver rolled down the window. The person waved me over with just one hand. I walked slowly up the stairs while sweating. When I got to the window, he opened the door for me to hop into the front seat. I quickly hopped into the front seat to see a brown-skinned man with slick-back hair. He was wearing a striped suit with a red tie to match. I stared at him with wide eyes and decided to ask him if he had bailed me out. He nodded after my question and rolled up the window. I closed the door, and we sat for a second.

"You could have used that 500,000 dollars for other things," I told him while moving my hair back. He laughed while his hand rested on the steering wheel, saying, "I could use my money for other things," in a French accent. He pulled out a white envelope from the side of the car and handed it to me. I opened the envelope to see a check for 1,000,000 dollars. We looked at each other, and he smiled. "Artasque!" I blurted it out. He laughed, "Never get into strangers' cars," as he buckled his seat belt. I buckled my seat belt after him and put the check in my lap. "But I didn't get the painting." I asked with a surprised look. "Yes, you didn't get the painting," he said.

I would be arrested during the same time period Solari was, but for different reasons. The officer saw Lee's injury and looked at the cameras to see that Solari had shot him. Then he went back to the painting that Solari was trying to get off the wall. He explained that she realized that Eddison had found a way to make fake copies of the one painting. The officer noticed that the painting was the one that he stole in 1995. I would find out that Eddison was being tried the same week. "I didn't want you to suffer for his issues," he said out loud to me. "What about Alex?" I asked, looking out the window. He explained that Alex was the one who voted against Eddison. He never liked him because he was jealous of his success. It was never his idea to frame me; he just wanted to steal the painting. He dropped me off at an interesting high-rise building in the middle of the city. "Look at that; it's finally rebuilt," he said while looking at it from his seat. I asked him if that was his house. "No, it was my brother's place," he said as he got in the car to open the door for me. He said that it was just a visit, and he was actually born in France. "My brother fell in love and moved to Las Vegas in the 70s," he said as he closed the door. I stood in front of the door to the first floor from outside. A doorman walked outside to greet him and me. "Greetings, Mr. Flamino and Ms. Flamino," the doorman said. I looked at Artasque with wide eyes and back at the doorman. He laughed. "Oh, I forgot to mention I'm your uncle," he said as he patted my back.

I told him that we had a lot of catching up to do. I met up with Valeria, who was planning on running away to Germany with her new boyfriend to go to college there and use her money to buy new clothes. Caddock was able to bribe his way back into his life as a famous wrestler, and I ended up attending one of his shows. He ended up getting me and Valeria front-row seats. Lee survived his bullet wound, but he would be bandaged on his right leg for months. He told me he had cut off all contact with Fanannah. Solari hadn't been released from prison for trying to kill Lee. But we don't mind that because I invited him to my new loft. I am finally in a relationship after all of these years. Lastly, I was able to get the real painting from my father back because of my uncle. He decided to hand it over to me instead of taking it back to France.

I was able to host my own art gallery at the same auction center in 1995. It was mostly to sell paintings inspired by my dad's work. Yes, curtains did drop, but it was mostly because Lee was working the curtain changes. I don't know when the public will like me again; I don't know when they stopped liking my father. I don't know when criminals like Eddison are liked more than me. I don't know why I had to change my last name. The only thing I know now is that once someone asked me why my name was Flamingo. I know the answer now because birds can fly. Flamingos can fly, but they didn't want me to fly like them.